Using Accountancy Software in Business

Using Accountancy Software in Business

Max Havard and P.K. McBride

Heinemann Professional Publishing Ltd
22 Bedford Square, London WC1B 3HH

LONDON   MELBOURNE   JOHANNESBURG   AUCKLAND

First published 1987

© *Max Harvard and P. K. McBride 1987*

British Library Cataloguing in Publication Data
Harvard, M. and McBride, P.K.
Using accountancy software in business
1. Accounting – Data processing
657' .95 '028553   HF5679

ISBN 0 434 91238 7

Designed by John Clark and Associates, Ringwood, Hampshire
Typeset by Express Typesetters, Farnham, Surrey

Printed and bound in Great Britain by
Dotesios Printers Ltd, Bradford-on-Avon, Wiltshire.

Contents

Foreword	7
Chapter 1 The Variety of Small Businesses	9
Chapter 2 Double-entry Bookkeeping – The Ledger System	15
Debit and Credit	16
Books of Account	29
Heather's Cafe	34
Palfreman Motor Spares	45
A Partnership at Work	54
The Limited Company	64
Small is Beautiful	73
Chapter 3 End of Period Accounts	81
The Trial Balance	81
Manufacturing Accounts	88
The Trading Account	96
The Profit and Loss Account	104
End of Period Adjustments	110
Appropriation Accounts	116
The Balance Sheet	126

Contents

Chapter 4 Stock Control 135

    Stock Valuations 136
    Economic Stock Levels 138
    Reorder and Safety Stock Levels 140
    Stock Control and the Computer 141

Chapter 5 The Interpretation of Accounts 143

Chapter 6 Sundry Considerations 157

    Value Added Tax 157
    Depreciation 167
    The Treatment of Hire Purchase 171

Chapter 7 Accountancy Software and your Accounts 177

    Organising your Accounts 178
    The Transfer to the Computer 179

Glossary 183

Index 189

Foreword

Making good use of accountancy software within your business is not difficult as long as you have good software and a reasonable understanding of accountancy practice. There are a number of good accounts packages on the market today. We believe the best of these, in terms of reliability, ease of use and sheer value for money, are those from Sagesoft. Their 'Popular Accounts' packages for the Amstrad PCW computers, and 'Bookkeeper' , 'Accountant', and 'Financial Controller' for PCs differ in price and in the scope of the facilities that they offer, but all have a common approach and a common core.

The packages have been designed with business people, not computer specialists, in mind and are specifically intended for use in small to medium sized businesses. Their clear layouts, logical structure and thorough error-trapping routines make them quick to learn and easy to use; and they are all based on the standard three ledgers (Sales, Purchase and Nominal) and double-entry system of bookkeeping. If you are already using this system for your accounts, then the transition from manual bookkeeping to computerised accounts will be simple and straightforward.

If you have been using a cash book, one of the single ledger systems, or have put everything into a shoebox and handed it to an accountant at the end of the year (it's one way to cope with the accounts!) then this

Foreword

book should help you to understand enough about the concepts and methods of accountancy to be able to make full use of Sage accountancy software in your business.

Those aspects of the accounts that are covered here can be handled by all of the Sage packages, except that the Balance Sheet and Stock Control facilities are not available on the entry level 'Bookkeeper' package for PCs. Anyone using this software and wanting these facilities can easily transfer to the 'Accountant' or 'Financial Controller' at any time in the future. The data files produced by 'Bookkeeper' are fully compatible with the higher level packages.

1

The Variety of Small Businesses

If there is one thing typical about small businesses, it is that few of them are typical!

Small businesses are run by individuals, and over time their managers will develop their own individual methods of handling their accounts. Most will find that when they decide to computerise, the main problem lies in adapting their existing accounting system to fit into the standard three-ledger mould. From there, however, it should be an easy step to transfer it to the computer.

Anyone running a business has to develop a sensible system for storing, maintaining and keeping their records. Many businesses simply retain all receipts and invoices and hand them all over to the accountant to sort out at the end of the year. Although this system certainly works and requires very little effort on the part of the manager, it is an expensive solution to the problem. But keeping your accounts in an organised fashion need not be either difficult or time-consuming. Recording data can be easy as long as the problem is approached in a logical and methodical way, and computerised accounting is accurate, easy to follow and much quicker to operate than any manual system.

The Variety of Small Business

Many small business owners are cautious about the computer and the role it may have in their business, and this caution is justifiable. A poor choice of hardware or software, or inadequate planning when the system is installed can all create difficulties and may have serious long-term consequences. Against that, a good system, properly installed, can be a boon to a business, taking the grind out of bookkeeping and offering opportunities for cost-saving. It will go beyond a manual system, taking the analyses of accounts and extending them to give forecasts of future trends. In today's highly competitive commercial climate, it is essential not only to have good information on the past and the present, but also on the future.

The IBM PC, Amstrad PC (and other quality PC clones), or the Amstrad PCW are all sensible choices for a small business. The hardware is well proven and capable of expansion as your business grows. At the very least, the system must have two floppy disk drives, but for greater efficiency and speed of operation a hard disk is advisable. Where several people are involved in the firm's clerical work – perhaps in Sales, Office Administration and Stock Control – then a network of PCs can be set up. If you are likely to need more than one computer – now or in the foreseeable future – talk to your local dealer about networked systems. You will be surprised at how cheap they can be.

Sagesoft's Financial Controller is the ideal accountancy software for PC users. It is adaptable, efficient, highly reliable and backed by the resources of a large and successful firm. You will find that it is flexible enough to suit your individual requirements, and the accounting structure is capable of easy alteration should your circumstances change in the future. Novices in the field will appreciate the fact that with Financial Controller you do not have to commit the whole of your accounts to the computer in one fell swoop. It can be done a stage at a time, leaving those areas which you do not fully understand, or where major changes from your existing procedures are needed, until you have gained experience and confidence.

With this book to help you to understand the accounting principles and practices that underlie the software, and the Sage User Manuals to guide you through the details of installation, you will have all you need for successful computerisation of your business.

Given the infinite variety of small businesses, it is simply not possible to cover every trading situation and accountancy method in this – or any – book. We have, therefore, set up a selection of sample businesses

The Variety of Small Business

which between them should provide examples of most of the situations that can occur.

The Cash Retailer

The majority of small businesses fall into this category, and with current trends this is likely to remain so. The cash retailer requires an accounting system which is capable of coping with a large number of one-off cash sales. Credit sales are unlikely to play a significant part in the accounts.

While cash retailers vary dramatically in the products that they sell, the accounting concepts and methods are much the same for them all. The newsagent selling papers, magazines, sweets and tobacco, the fish and chip shop dealing in food and canned drinks, the boutique, the butcher and the flower shop. All of these face the same problems in recording purchases, sales and expense, and in drawing these together into an organised set of accounts.

Our example here is Heather's Café. Heather's is a one-woman business, with limited expenses and a fairly low turnover. Her sales are all cash, and her creditors few. We have deliberately avoided any complications here, so that we can focus on the principles behind the accounting structures and practices.

The Distributor

Although the distributor will almost certainly have a more complex accounting system than the cash retailer, it may well prove simpler to computerise. The typical distributor will buy in goods, on credit, from a number of different suppliers; sales will also be largely on credit and to a limited set of known customers. ('Limited' may mean several hundred or more, but this should be contrasted with the cash retailer who may serve several thousand different customers in the course of a year.) As the business will almost certainly be using a sales and purchase ledger system already, the transition to a ledger-based computer system should not require too much reorganisation of the accounts.

Palfreman Motor Spares is our example distributor. Again this is a sole trader operation. In these accounts we will look at credit sales, the return of goods and stock control systems.

The Variety of Small Business

The Wholesaler

Wholesalers have changed their role over the years. In the past they were seen as middlemen between the manufacturers and retailers, but now many open their doors to the public. To highlight this change in the trade, our example in this area is a Cash and Carry wholesale outlet.

Two-Tone Cash & Carry is a partnership, and a significantly larger business than the earlier two. New points introduced here include partnership finances, the ownership of premises and coping with carriage charges.

The Manufacturer

The accounting systems in manufacturing firms are necessarily rather different from those of businesses that revolve around buying and selling — whether at retail or wholesale level. The valuation of stock and costings of labour, plant, research and development are the most obvious areas of difference, but by no means the only ones.

While the greatest volume of manufactured goods in this country are produced by large concerns, there are very many small manufacturers, particularly in the craft and also the high technology and fashion fields. The products of the latter tend to have shorter life-spans than those of mainstream manufacturing; and the firms may also be transitory. Our sample firm, Grunks, represents these manufacturers, producing fashionable ephemera.

Grunks Ltd is a limited company and thus raises the matter of shares, dividends and directors' fees. It also gives us the opportunity to examine the very special accounting needs of manufacturers.

The Service Industries

After retailing, the second largest group of small businesses covers those in the service sector — domestic and office cleaning, repairs, hairdressers, beauticians, job agencies, insurance brokers, estate agents and similar; a whole range of firms that can be started by almost anyone with the necessary skills and enterprise. Unlike the earlier businesses, these generally require comparatively little starting capital.

The Variety of Small Business

In Sue's Beauty Salon we will deal not just with the particular requirements of the service industries, but also look into depreciation and discount, and the concept of 'stock' amongst other things. As the Salon is organised as a limited company – though on a much smaller scale than Grunks Ltd – it will give us another view of company accounts.

2

Double-entry Bookkeeping – The Ledger System

The purpose of any accounting system is to record transactions and to provide information about the business. It must be able to tell you:

- The amounts owed to suppliers of goods and services.
- The amounts owed by customers for goods received or work done.
- The total sales and purchase during a period.
- The cost of expenses incurred in running the business – e.g. rent, rates, power, salaries.
- The value of cash in hand and at the bank.
- The value of the business's capital assets – land, buildings, equipment, vehicles.

You will see that most of these amounts and values will have to be calculated and with a manual system that is going to take time. With Sage accounts packages, as with all good software systems, all of the calculations are done for you. Most of the totals and values in this set will be brought up to date as each new transaction is posted; others are updated during end-of-period routines.

With a manual system, the accountant, or the firm's manager or owner, can use this basic information to produce a range of financial statements

Double-entry Bookkeeping – The Ledger System

and summaries. A comprehensive computerised system will produce most or all of this for you. The most important of these outputs are:

- A Trading and Profit and Loss Account, to show the overall trading position. Is the business making a profit, and if so how much?
- A Balance Sheet showing the assets and liabilities of the firm.
- Departmental analyses of profit and loss.
- Statements comparing expenses and income at different times.
- VAT returns.

We will return to these outputs from the system in the next section, but before that, let us look at the way in which transactions are recorded in a double-entry bookkeeping system.

Debit and Credit

The key concepts in double-entry bookkeeping are those of separate records of account for each part of the financial system, and of *Debit* and *Credit*. Thus a separate account is kept for each supplier and customer, for each category of expenses, for total sales and purchases of different types of stock.

In very simple terms, the basis of the Debit and Credit concept is that the movement of money into one account – one part of the system – will always be balanced by an outward movement elsewhere. When new goods are bought in, the value in the stock account will be increased, but the amount in the cash account will be reduced by an equivalent amount.

It is called double-entry bookkeeping because every transaction is recorded twice – once as a debit in one account and once as a credit in another.

Suppose you kept detailed records of your household finance. Then, if you bought a £2 jar of coffee, it would be recorded as a Credit of £2 in the Cash Account, and a Debit of £2 in the Coffee Account. It counts as a Credit to the cash account, because if it were returned to the shop, the £2 would be returned. Similarly, it counts as a Debit to the Coffee Account, because that £2 is 'owed' to the cash account.

Let's see how this works at a business level. In a manual system, each ledger page is split into two columns, with debits recorded on the left, and credits on the right. So, when Heather stocks up on coffee for her café, the transaction will be recorded as shown here.

```
          BANK ACCOUNT                        COFFEE ACCOUNT
    Debit      │   Credit              Debit       │    Credit
       £       │      £                   £        │       £
   ════════    │  ════════            ════════     │   ════════
               │ Coffee  24.00        Cash  24.00  │
```

This shows a loss of £24 from the Bank Account (Credit £24 marked to Coffee) and in return there is a gain of £24 in the Coffee Account (Debit £24 marked to Bank).

Obviously the transactions in any real books of accounts are going to be more complex, both in monetary terms and in the way in which they are recorded. However, the basic concept remains the same.

For every gain (Debit) there must be a corresponding loss (Credit).

We can now introduce three more fundamental accountancy terms: *Assets, Liabilities and Capital.*

Assets

An asset is something which we own, or which is owed to us. At a domestic level, the jar of coffee that we bought is an asset, as is the cash remaining in our pockets and bank accounts. The assets of a business are usually divided into *Fixed Assets* – those of more or less constant value, such as buildings, equipment and vehicles; and *Current Assets* – those that fluctuate with trading, for example stock, cash in the bank and monies owed by customers.

Double-entry Bookkeeping – The Ledger System

Assets are written on the Debit (left) side of the records of account. For example, Smith & Jones spent £15,000 on furniture and £8,000 on a car when they started up their business.

```
      FURNITURE & FITTINGS AC.              MOTOR CAR ACCOUNT
            £           £                       £            £
Bank    15,000                        Bank    8,000
```

These entries will, of course, be balanced by Credit entries elsewhere in the books. Both of these will have corresponding entries in the Bank Account record.

```
                    BANK ACCOUNT
                       £                         £
           c/f      22,000
                                   F & F      15,000
                                   Motor Car   8,000
```

Liabilities

Liabilities are the amounts owed by a business – its *debts*. Sums due to suppliers, mortgages, bank loans and overdrafts are all liabilities. They are normally divided into two groups; monies owed in taxes or to customers, bank overdrafts and other debts that change with trading are all *Current Liabilities*; while loans, share capital and other long term debts are grouped under the heading 'Financed By'.

Double-entry Bookkeeping – The Ledger System

In the records of account, these items appear on the Credit (right) side. Look what happens to that Bank Account when we bring it up to date. The £22,000 that Smith & Jones started with is not enough to cover the two purchases.

```
                    BANK ACCOUNT
                £                              £
    c/f      22,000
                         F & F           15,000
                         Motor Car        8,000
                                         ──────
                                          1,000
```

The £1,000 overdraft at the bank is a *Liability*.

Capital

The term *'Capital'* is used loosely to mean several slightly different things. When a business is first started, Capital refers to the money put into it – usually by the owners – to get things going. A loan from a bank for development purposes is sometimes referred to as 'Working Capital', though strictly speaking this term should be reserved for the excess of Current Assets over Current Liabilities.

In an on-going business, Capital can be defined as the excess of Assets over Liabilities; but it is itself a liability, for Capital is the money owed by the business to its owners. The equation can be shown in two ways:

    Capital = Assets – Liabilities

and

    Assets = Liabilities + Capital

This will always be true, for in double-entry bookkeeping; every transaction affects both sides of the equation equally.

Double-entry Bookkeeping – The Ledger System

When Smith & Jones started their partnership, Smith put in £12,000 and Jones invested £10,000. These sums appeared in the Capital Account as liabilities, though they are assets in the bank account.

```
                    CAPITAL ACCOUNT
          £                            £
                        Bank (Smith)  12,000
                        Bank (Jones)  10,000

                     BANK ACCOUNT
                    £                  £
Capital (Smith) 12,000
Capital (Jones) 10,000
```

At this stage the business has a Capital of £22,000 (Smith + Jones), Assets of £23,000 (Car + Furniture) and Liabilities of £1,000 (Bank Overdraft).

£22,000 = £23,000 − £1,000

Capital = Assets − Liabilities

The assets, liabilities and capital of a business will fluctuate over time. Take, for example, a business which buys two machines for its factory at a cost of £3,000 each. The purchases are recorded in a special account.

```
                 EQUIPMENT ACCOUNT
                            £              £
Bank (Machine 1)        3,000
Bank (Machine 2)        3,000
```

Double-entry Bookkeeping – The Ledger System

Its assets in machinery are now worth £6,000, but demand for the product decreases and one of the machines is sold for its purchase price. (The complexities of depreciation, second-hand value and inflation can safely be left until later.)

EQUIPMENT ACCOUNT

	£		£
Bank (Machine 1)	3,000		
Bank (Machine 2)	3,000	Bank (Machine 2)	3,000

We can see that we now have an Equipment Account with £6,000 Debit and £3,000 Credit, which means that our net machines assets are £6,000 − £3,000 = £3,000.

In this second example, the business has an overdraft of £2,000, and recieves a cheque from a client for £1,200. The 'bank account' – and by this we mean the record in his books, not those of the Bank – will show this.

BANK ACCOUNT

	£		£
Sales	1,200	Balance	2,000

The new position at the bank is Debit (Plus) £1,200 less Credit (Minus) £2,000 = £800 Credit balance. The overdraft, a Liability, has been decreased.

Lastly, look at this partnership. It was started by Green and Brown who each put in £2,000 capital.

CAPITAL ACCOUNT

	£		£
		Bank (Green)	2,000
		Bank (Brown)	2,000

Double-entry Bookkeeping – The Ledger System

It soon became obvious that the business needed more investment if it was to succeed, and each of the partners put in a further £1,000.

```
                      CAPITAL ACCOUNT
          £         ||              £
                    || Bank (Green)  2,000
                    || Bank (Brown)  2,000
                    || Bank (Green)  1,000
                    || Bank (Brown)  1,000
```

The capital of the firm increased from £4,000 to £6,000. Conversely, if either or both of the partners withdrew some of their capital from the firm, this would be shown on the Debit side of the Capital account and the overall capital liability of the firm would be decreased.

Let's take a firm through its first few weeks of trading to see how these concepts work out in practice. In this example, we will record transactions as they would appear in a manual bookkeeping system. We will therefore have to record each as a debit and credit entry. (It is worth remembering that with Sage accountancy packages most of these 'double-entries' would only in fact be entered once – though the system will record each in two related accounts.)

Robin Goodfellow was a firm believer in the future of the Amstrad PC computers and set up a small PC Centre in his home town. Over the course of the first month there were the following transactions:

Double-entry Bookkeeping – The Ledger System

1. *Jan 1st: Robin started up the business with £10,000 capital. This was paid directly into the bank. The transactions were recorded.*

BANK ACCOUNT

Date		£	Date		£
Jan 1st	Capital	10,000			

CAPITAL ACCOUNT

Date		£	Date		£
			Jan 1st	Bank	10,000

The bank account has increased by £10,000 (Asset) and the Capital account shows a £10,000 Credit balance (Liability).

Note that the date and name of the other relevant account are included in each entry. If necessary they can be used to cross check any discrepancies that may occur. If you get discrepancies with Sage accountancy packages, it will indicate that either the data disk has been corrupted, or that you have given the wrong account reference number for the double-entry – and as the system displays the account name when you type in this number, this sort of error is simple to avoid. What you will not suffer from are those errors caused by copying figures wrongly from one account to another.

Double-entry Bookkeeping – The Ledger System

2 *Jan 3rd: Robin wrote a cheque for £800 to pay one month's rent for the premises.*

BANK ACCOUNT

Date		£	Date		£
Jan 1st	Capital	10,000			
			Jan 3rd	Rent	800

RENT & RATES ACCOUNT

Date		£	Date		£
Jan 3rd	Bank	800			

The bank account has been reduced by £800 and the Rent account has received this sum. We won't bother to keep a running check on the balance in the bank at this stage, for here we are focusing on the individual transactions.

3 *Jan 5th: The first stock arrives and is paid for by cheque.*

BANK ACCOUNT

Date		£	Date		£
Jan 1st	Capital	10,000			
			Jan 3rd	Rent	800
			Jan 5th	Purchase	2,000

PURCHASES ACCOUNT

Date		£	Date		£
Jan 5th	Bank	2,000			

Double-entry Bookkeeping – The Ledger System

Goods (stock) bought for resale are called *purchases* for the purposes of bookkeeping. When a purchase is made, the asset of stock will increase – here by £2,000 – and the money paid is taken out of the bank account by a Credit entry.

4 *Jan 8th: He pays £750 for a desk, chairs and display cabinets, which fall under the heading of Furniture and Fittings.*

BANK ACCOUNT

Date		£	Date		£
Jan 1st	Capital	10,000	Jan 3rd	Rent	800
			Jan 5th	Purchase	2,000
			Jan 8th	F & F	750

FURNITURE & FITTINGS ACCOUNT

Date		£	Date		£
Jan 8th	Bank (desk, etc)	750			

These assets appear on the left (Debit) side of the ledger page.

Double-entry Bookkeeping – The Ledger System

5 Jan 10th: Goodfellow's PC Centre is now open for trading, and it is not long before he has made his first sale – a small networked system and associated software for £3,000.

BANK ACCOUNT

Date		£	Date		£
Jan 1st	Capital	10,000	Jan 3rd	Rent	800
			Jan 5th	Purchase	2,000
			Jan 8th	F & F	500
Jan 10th	Sales	3,000			

SALES ACCOUNT

Date		£	Date		£
			Jan 8th	Bank	3,000

The sale of goods is recorded as a Credit entry in the Sales Account, for these goods have gone from the firm and are no longer an asset. The asset which replaces them is the £3,000 in the bank account.

6 Jan 13th: Another sale! But this time only £100's worth of software. Not as dramatic as the last, but there is plenty of profit for Robin in small sales as long as he can get enough of them. The money is paid in cash, which goes into the till.

CASH ACCOUNT

Date		£	Date		£
Jan 13th	Sales	100			

SALES ACCOUNT

Date		£	Date		£
			Jan 8th	Bank	3,000
			Jan 13th	Cash	100

Double-entry Bookkeeping — The Ledger System

7   *Jan 18th: Robin uses the cash account for many small payments. On this day, the shop cleaner wanted his wages.*

CASH ACCOUNT

Date		£	Date		£
Jan 13th	Sales	100			
			Jan 18th	Cleaning	15

CLEANING ACCOUNT

Date		£	Date		£
Jan 18th	Cash (Wages)	15			

This particular example raises the question of types of transactions needing separate records of account. Some are obvious. There must be distinct accounts for Sales, Purchases, money in the Bank and in Cash, and Capital. Others will depend upon the nature of the business. A single Equipment account may be sufficient where there is only a limited amount of equipment, but in another firm it may be useful to keep separate accounts for office equipment, plant, light machinery and tools. Likewise Robin Goodfellow may be better off including his cleaning costs in a General Expenses or Petty Cash account along with other minor items of expenditure.

8   *Jan 23rd: One of the display cabinets proved to be too small for the job and Robin was able to sell it to someone else without losing anything on the deal.*

BANK ACCOUNT

Date		£	Date		£
Jan 1st	Capital	10,000			
			Jan 3rd	Rent	800
			Jan 5th	Purchase	2,000
			Jan 8th	F & F	500
Jan 10th	Sales	3,000			
Jan 23rd	F & F	150			

27

Double-entry Bookkeeping – The Ledger System

FURNITURE & FITTINGS ACCOUNT

Date		£	Date		£
Jan 8th	Bank (desk,etc)	750	Jan 23rd	Bank (Cabinet)	150

Although goods have been sold, this transaction does not appear in the Sales Account but is written into Furniture and Fittings. This is because that display cabinet was not bought to resell at a profit – Robin is in the PC business, not office furniture.

The Sales Account is only used to record the selling of goods which have been expressly bought for resale – i.e. which were first recorded in the Purchases Account – and not for the sale of assets.

If you use Financial Controller, a Sale would normally be recorded via the Invoicing routine. As part of this, Financial Controller checks through the Stock Control module that the items to be sold are actually available. Therefore, any attempt to record this kind of transaction as a 'Sale' would fail as the display cabinet would not be present on the stock inventory.

SUMMARY

- Separate accounts are needed for different categories of transactions within a business.

- Every transaction is recorded in two ways – as a Debit in one account and as a Credit in another.

- Debits and Assets are written on the left of the ledger pages; Credits and Liabilities are written on the right.

- Capital counts as a Liability to the business, for it is money owed to the proprietor as an individual.

Double-entry Bookkeeping – The Ledger System

Books of account

In the last part we introduced the concept of the account (or record of account as it is sometimes called) as the place in which are recorded all the transactions relating to one category of income or expenditure. Now, even a small business will need a considerable number of accounts and so, for convenience, they are often grouped into *Books of Account* or *Ledgers.* All the Sage accountancy packages follow this convention.

The Purchase Ledger

Few businesses will buy all their stock from a single supplier and few will pay for their goods in cash or by cheque at the time of purchase. When goods are bought on credit, the business will owe money to another individual or company – it will have a *Creditor* – and this fact must be written into the books. Each supplier must have a separate account in which the debts, and their later settlements, are recorded. These accounts are grouped into the Purchase Ledger.

The Purchase Ledger should then be seen as a record of credit events over a period of time. It is here that the firm's manager will look to find the trading position with other companies; to see which suppliers must be paid, and how much and when.

It must be emphasised that the Purchase Ledger is essentially a collection of *Suppliers'* accounts. There will be another – more often several other – accounts that keep track of the purchases as a whole. Robin Goodfellow was using a single Purchases Account, but as his business grows he would do well to split this into Hardware Purchases and Software Purchases. These Purchases Accounts are totally seperate entites – *not* within the Purchase Ledger.

The second point that needs to be stressed is that the Purchase Ledger – and the Purchases Accounts – deal only with goods bought for resale. Any other expenses – postage, petrol, equipment, or whatever – whether bought by cash or on credit, are dealt with elsewhere.

Double-entry Bookkeeping – The Ledger System

Normally, in a manual system, the totals from the purchase ledger – how much is owing to each supplier – will be recorded into the overall Purchases Accounts on a regular basis – weekly or monthly. It is done in this way, rather than by recording each individual transaction here, so that the Purchases Accounts do not become cluttered up with excessive detail. We shall return to these very important accounts at a later stage.

The Sales Ledger

This should be seen as the mirror image of the Purchase Ledger, and is where the accounts of transactions with credit customers (*Debtors*) are maintained. At the end of each accounting period, totals from here will be transferred across to the Sales Accounts, so that these – like the Purchases Account – contain only summaries and overall totals for each category of sales transactions.

Day Books

Those businesses with large volumes of credit sales or purchases often use Day Books as a convenient way of collecting data. The *Sales and Sales Returns Day Book* will record the details of goods sold on credit. Each entry from here will then be posted daily to the debit side of the customers' accounts, while totals will be posted to the Sales Accounts at the end of each accounting period – usually one month. *Credit notes* sent to customers will also be recorded here in the first instance.

Double-entry Bookkeeping – The Ledger System

SALES DAY BOOK

Date	Details	£	£
Jan 12th	Grist the Millers Hardware Sage Accounts	799.95 149.95	949.90

SALES LEDGER
Grist the Millers Account

| Jan 12th | Computer Sales | 949.90 | | | |

COMPUTER SALES ACCOUNT

| | | Jan 12th | Grist | 949.90 |

Similarly, a *Purchases* and *Purchases Returns* Day Book can be used for recording details of invoices sent to suppliers. The data stored here will be posted to the suppliers' accounts in the Purchase Ledger and to the Purchases Accounts.

It should be noted that these Day Books are not part of the double entry bookkeeping system, but simply books of memoranda that record details of transactions.

The Day Book routines in the accounts packages are not used for data entry – there is no point – but serve a valuable function in that they allow you to extract details of trading during a given period. For example, the Day Book print-outs can be used to view all the sales in the previous month.

* SALES and Purchase Ledger = Personal (Suppliers) Customers

Double-entry Bookkeeping – The Ledger System

The Nominal Ledger

This is sometimes referred to as the *General Ledger* or the *Impersonal Ledger*. (In contrast to the Sales and Purchases Ledgers which are Personal in the sense that they relate to individual suppliers and customers.) All the other accounts are maintained here, including Sales and Purchases, Bank, Cash, Wages, Rent & Rates and all other expenses, the debtors and creditors of the business, Plant, Machinery, Property, Capital and others relating to assets and liabilites.

This ledger is the centre of the accounting system, and indeed where there are no credit sales or purchases, a business can run on the Nominal Ledger alone.

It is from the information stored in the Nominal Ledger that the accountant (or the software after you have computerised) will draw up the *Trial Balance*, *Trading and Profit and Loss Account* and *Balance Sheet*, as well as a variety of financial summaries.

Perhaps it's in the name – 'Nominal' is not a word that carries much immediate significance – but this ledger is frequently one of the least understood parts of the accounting system. There is no reason why this should be so. For the moment, just think of the Nominal Ledger as being the place where the accounts are written, for that is its main purpose. We will tackle its other functions later as we come to them.

The Cash Book

Many small businesses with manual systems do not use a Nominal Ledger. But all business do need – in some form or other – a Cash Book.

In the examples given so far, we have used separate Bank and Cash Accounts. In manual systems, these are normally combined within a Cash Book. This will record the money received by the business and its outgoings. At the end of each accounting period, the balance of cash in hand and at the bank will be calculated and recorded here as well.

The Cash Book has a slightly different format from that of simple accounts, in that each side of the ledger has two columns – one for Cash and one for Bank.

Double-entry Bookkeeping – The Ledger System

This is, of course, due to the fact that the Cash Book replaces the two separate accounts.

If you are used to a Cash Book system, then it will be necessary to split it into its two component accounts when transferring the accounts to the computer.

In the next few sections we shall see how our five sample businesses handle their data. We will do this by following each one's transactions over a month, and looking at the relevant accounts at the end of that time. In these, we will start by using a manual accounting system, as the underlying structure may be clearer that way, and as readers may well be familiar with this to a greater or lesser extent. Later we will look at what would be needed to transfer these accounts to an accountancy package. Pay particular attention to the business or businesses that are closest to your own, and notice the way in which their accounts are organised.

SUMMARY

- The *Purchase Ledger* holds suppliers' accounts. Matching entries for transactions with suppliers are recorded in the *Purchases Account*.

- The *Sales Ledger* holds customers' accounts. The matching entries for these transactions are in the *Sales Account*.

- *Day Books* are a convenient way of collecting records of transactions together before transferring them to the appropriate accounts. In the Sage accounts systems, the Day Books are listings of transactions of a given type during a given period.

- The *Nominal Ledger* is where all accounts, except those of individual suppliers and customers, are kept.

- The *Cash Book* holds the Cash and Bank Accounts. It does not exist as a separate entity in the Sage accounting structure. There these two accounts are held within the Nominal Ledger.

Double-entry Bookkeeping – The Ledger System

Heather's Café

Heather's Café is very typical of so many new small businesses. It is owned and run by one person, with a little waged help. Its sales are entirely cash over the counter, and its purchases a mixture of cash and credit, but from only a few suppliers.

She does not need a particularly complex accounting system, but like all business people, she must be able to keep track of the comings and goings of money. This is not just for the benefit of the Inland Revenue, but so that she can see how the business is performing, and perhaps find ways of improving its efficiency.

The Transactions
1. Jan 1st. Start business with £8,000 capital in the bank.
2. Jan 2nd. Pay rent of £1,000.
3. Jan 3rd. Buy Furniture on credit – £2,000.
4. Jan 4th. Buy foodstuffs on credit – £1,400.
5. Jan 5th. Pay for advertising – £80.
6. Jan 8th. Buy cleaning equipment on credit – £200.
7. Jan 9th. Withdraw some cash from bank – £150.
8. Jan 11th. Record cash sales to date – £175.
9. Jan 14th. Pay wages in cash – £80.
10. Jan 16th. Minor purchase – £10.
11. Jan 18th. Record cash sales – £900.
12. Jan 21st. Pay cash into bank – £800.
13. Jan 24th. Draw cash for own use – £120.
14. Jan 25th. Record cash sales – £1,100.
15. Jan 28th. Pay cash into bank – £1,000.
16. Jan 30th. Pay foodstuffs bill – £1,400.
17. Jan 30th. Restock on foodstuffs – £1,700.

Double-entry Bookkeeping — The Ledger System

Heather's Cafe
Accounts as at Jan 31st.

CAPITAL ACCOUNT

Date	Details	£	Date	Details	£
(1)			Jan 1	Bank	8,000

This is much the same as we have seen earlier. The £8,000 capital that is paid into the bank is recorded as a Credit entry — a liability — in the Capital Account. Look ahead to the Cash Book page and you will find that it has been recorded as a Debit in the Bank column there.

RENT ACCOUNT

Date	Details	£	Date	Details	£
(2) Jan 2	Bank	1,000			

Here we have a Debit entry in the Rent account, matched by a Credit in the Bank column of the Cash Book. We now have rented premises as an asset instead of money in the bank.

FIXTURES & FITTINGS ACCOUNT

Date	Details	£	Date	Details	£
(3) Jan 3	Roberts	2,000			

ROBERTS ACCOUNT

Date	Details	£	Date	Details	£
(3)			Jan 3	Fix & Fits	2,000

Heather bought various items including freezers, cookers, tables and chairs. Each type or individual item could have been allocated its own account, but in practice it makes far more sense to group like assets into a single account under a suitable heading.

Double-entry Bookkeeping – The Ledger System

This transaction is different from the earlier two in that it does not affect the Cash Book at this stage. The furniture was bought from Roberts on credit, not by cash or cheque. So, while Heather has 'gained' assets – her furniture – the 'loser' has not been the bank, but Roberts. The debt is recorded in his account. When the cheque is paid – next month – the payment will be recorded as a Debit in this account, and a Credit in the Bank column of the Cash Book.

PURCHASES ACCOUNT

	Date	Details	£	Date	Details	£
(4)	Jan 4	Davies	1 400			
(17)	Jan 30	Davies	1 700			
		Balance	3 100			

(Purchase Ledger)

DAVIES ACCOUNT

	Date	Details	£	Date	Details	£
(4)				Jan 4	Purchases	1 400
(16)	Jan 30	Bank	1 400	Jan 30	Purchases	1 700
(17)		Balance	1 700			
			3 100			3 100
					Balance	1 700

There are several points to notice in these slightly more complicated pages.

- The foodstuffs that Heather buys for the Café count as Purchases, as these are goods bought for resale.
- You will see that the transactions are recorded in the two accounts in exactly the same way as the deal with Roberts. When the first bill is paid by cheque on January 30th, this is recorded as a Debit in the Davies Account, and a Credit in the Cash book.
- The end of the month totals in the Purchases and Davies Accounts are the same, but only because Heather has bought all of her foodstuffs from there. When she starts to use other suppliers as well, there will no longer be this simple link. What we should expect then is that the sum of all foods suppliers' accounts should be the same as the Purchases.

Double-entry Bookkeeping – The Ledger System

■ When the accounts are made up at the end of the month, the difference between the total Debits (£1,400) and Credits (£3,100) is recorded as a Balance on the Debit side, so that the final totals are the same. This sum is also entered as a new starting balance on the Credit side beneath the double line. It is the record of an outstanding debt.

ADVERTISING ACCOUNT

	Date	Details	£	Date	Details	£
(5)	Jan 5	Bank	80			

A simple transaction, with the £80 cheque for advertising being recorded here and in the Cash Book.

CLEANING ACCOUNT

	Date	Details	£	Date	Details	£
(6)	Jan 8	Whiting	200			

WHITING ACCOUNT

	Date	Details	£	Date	Details	£
(6)				Jan 8	Cleaning	200

Another straightforward credit transaction as Heather acquires cleaning equipment for her Café. She is here using a separate account for cleaning, rather than incorporating it in general expenses, as the nature of her business means that cleaning costs are relatively high. It emphasises the point that separate accounts are needed for categories of expenditure if they are a significant proportion of the business expenses. What is 'significant' depends upon the size of the business. A few pounds a week are insignificant to a small firm, while even £200 would hardly merit a distinct account in a large one.

Double-entry Bookkeeping – The Ledger System

SALES ACCOUNT

Date	Details	£	Date	Details	£
(8)			Jan 11	Cash	175
(11)			Jan 18	Cash	900
(14)			Jan 25	Cash	1,100
				Balance	2,175

The sales side of Heather's accounts is simpler than the purchase side as all sales are in cash. The till money is counted periodically and recorded here and in the Cash Book – each of these entries has its equivalent there. It is recorded as a Debit in the Cash Account and a Credit in the Sales Account – she now has money in place of the goods.

The Balance here represents the end of the month total for this account.

WAGES ACCOUNT

Date	Details	£	Date	Details	£
(9) Jan 14	Cash	80			

This records a simple transaction, receiving labour for money. Look for its balancing entry in the Credit side of the Cash Book.

SUNDRY EXPENSES ACCOUNT

Date	Details	£	Date	Details	£
(10) Jan 16	Cash	10			

When Heather stocked up on light bulbs, she decided that it really wasn't worth creating a separate Light Bulb Account – the amount spent on these items over a year is just not that much. Instead, the transaction is recorded in a Sundry Expenses Account. (It will, of course, also appear as a Credit entry in the Cash Book.)

Double-entry Bookkeeping – The Ledger System

DRAWINGS ACCOUNT

Date	Details	£	Date	Details	£
(13) Jan 24	Cash	120			

Drawings refer to those monies taken from the business by the owner for his or her own purposes – generally living expenses. They are not included in the Wages account, as in accounting the owner is treated differently from any employee.

CASH BOOK

Date	Debits	Cash £	Bank £	Date	Credits	Cash £	Bank £
(1) Jan 1	Capital		8,000				
(2)				Jan 2	Rent		1,000
(5)				Jan 5	Advertising		80
(7) Jan 9	Bank	150		Jan 9	Cash		150
(8) Jan 11	Sales	175					
(9)				Jan 14	Wages	80	
(10)				Jan 16	Sundries	10	
(11) Jan 18	Sales	1,400					
(12) Jan 21	Cash		800	Jan 21	Bank	800	
(13)				Jan 24	Drawings	120	
(14) Jan 25	Sales	600					
(15) Jan 28	Cash		1,000	Jan 28	Bank	1,000	
(16)				Jan 30	Davies		1,400
					Balance	315	7,170
		2,325	9,800			2,325	9,800
		======	======			======	======
	Balance	315	7,170				

Almost all of the entries in the Cash Book have already been dealt with in the comments on the individual accounts. Only three remain, and they are those of January 9th (7), 21st (12) and 28th (15), where money is transferred between the Cash and Bank columns.

On January 9th, Heather drew £150 in cash from the bank. This is therefore recorded by a Debit entry in the cash columns, as it is an asset to Cash – and the comment 'Bank' shows where it came from. On the Credit side it is written into the Bank column, with the comment 'Cash' showing where it went. The payments into the bank of £800 and £1,000 in cash are recorded similarly.

39

Double-entry Bookkeeping – The Ledger System

Once all the entries have been made for the accounting period, it is necessary to balance the accounts. By adding up the entries on each side we can see the net effect of the transactions on the individual accounts. The difference between them is the balance. Some will have only Debit entries – here, the Purchases, General Expenses, Wages and Drawings accounts are such; others will have only Credit entries – here, this is true of Sales. The remaining accounts have entries on both the Debit and Credit sides – in this instance, the suppliers accounts and the Cash Book.

If we look at the Cash columns of the Cash Book, we will find that the money coming in (Debit) totals £2,325, while the money going out (Credit) totals £2,010. There is a difference of £315.

In the Bank columns the total coming in – from starting Capital and payments into the bank – was £9,800, while the Debits totalled only £2,630. This leaves a balance of £7,170.

The £7,170 (Bank) and £315 (Cash) sums are first shown as balances on the Credit side – so that the totals in the columns on both sides are the same. They are then 'carried down' to the next accounting period – next month – where they will appear as the first Debit entries. This shows that we actually have cash and money in the bank. A credit balance in the Bank Account would indicate an overdraft.

Accounts can be balanced at any time – the Sage systems maintain a running balance on all accounts – but they must all be balanced at the end of the accounting period. Scan back through all the other accounts, and you will see that – with the exception of those containing only one entry – they have been totalled and balanced. In every account with entries on both sides, the difference – marked 'balance' – has been added into the smaller total, and carried down to the next period.

You will see in Chapter 3 how these balances are used in the next stage of the accounting process, the production of the Trial Balance.

Double-entry Bookkeeping – The Ledger System

SUMMARY

- The names used for accounts are a matter of personal choice, though there are some accounts which almost all businesses identify in the same way – e.g. Purchases, Sales, Drawings, Cash, Bank.

- When a transaction is recorded, each entry should be marked with a reference to the other account that handles it.

- At the end of the accounting period – normally a month – the entries in each account are totalled. If the sums on the two sides are not the same, the balance is carried on to the next period.

The transfer to computer

After one month's trading, the basic shape of the business is beginning to emerge. There have been no credit sales, and Heather intends that there will not be any. She will therefore need no Sales Ledger accounts for customers. At this stage, she is only buying on credit from one supplier, but she may use a few more in future. If she allows for 10 accounts in the Purchase Ledger, this should be more than enough to handle any credit suppliers during the year. Lastly, she has so far created 15 other accounts, but there will no doubt be some other categories of expenses that have yet to emerge. She should leave plenty of space in setting up the Nominal Ledger.

So, when Heather runs the Initialisation routine (in the Utilities menu) she will specify:

```
SALES      0
PURCHASE  10
NOMINAL   40
```

As blank accounts take up virtually no disk space, there is no harm – and much sense – in specifying for far more than you think you need.

The next stage is to set up the *Nominal Accounts*. The key ones – marked * in the list below – are covered in the Initialisation routine; the others are opened through 'Nominal Accounts' in the 'Nominal Ledger Postings' menu.

Double-entry Bookkeeping – The Ledger System

The Debtors' Control account holds the total of all amounts outstanding in customers' accounts in the Sales Ledger. Similarly, the Creditors' Control account shows the total owing on the suppliers' accounts in the Purchases Ledger. These control accounts must be present before the other ledgers can be used.

The Tax Control account is where all VAT charges – on both Inputs and Outputs – will be recorded by the system.

One nominal account will be needed for each category of expense, as with a manual system, though Roberts and Whiting – to whom she owes money for furniture and cleaning equipment – are probably best dealt with in a single account labelled 'Sundry Creditors'. There will be so few transactions with these that they scarcely merit separate accounts.

The simplest approach is to follow the numbering system suggested in the User Manual in the section on the Nominal Ledger. (Note that the numbers used in this book are geared to the larger nominal ledgers of the Accoutant and Financial Controller. They would need to be altered for the other packages, where the highest number is 999.) The basis of this is that accounts of the same type should have adjacent numbers.

There are several routines in the packages where sets of accounts can be handled as single entities for calculation or print-out. These sets are defined by giving a range of account numbers. Thus the range 3000 to 3210 would cover all Expenses.

```
   0003 Furniture & Fittings    2001 Purchases
   0035 Stock                   3000 Drawings
*  0038 Debtors' Control        3001 Salaries
*  0065 Creditors' Control      3010 Rent
   0066 Sundry Creditors        3020 Rates
*  0069 Tax Control             3080 Cleaning
*  0088 Cash                    3180 Advertising
*  0089 Bank                    3210 Sundries
   0095 Capital
   1000 Sales
   1099 Discount
```

More Nominal accounts will be needed as the year goes on, but they can be added at any time.

Double-entry Bookkeeping – The Ledger System

There is just one account to set up in the Purchase Ledger, and that is for Roberts. Once the name and other details have been entered – in the 'Purchase Accounts' routine – Heather can turn to the 'Postings' menu. Here she should select 'Invoices' and give the details of the transactions on the 14th and 30th. The settlement of the 30th can then be recorded under 'Payments'. That is all that is needed in the Purchase Ledger for this month. We can now move on to the Nominal Ledger.

Many transactions need only a single entry in one of the Cash or Bank Receipts or Payments routines. The balancing entry will be made in the account specified. So, to record the transfer of Capital to the bank, Heather will need to go to the Bank Payments section. There she will give the reference number of the Capital account, the date of the transaction and the amount. When the entry is posted, a credit of £8,000 will be written into the Capital account as well as a debit of £8,000 in the bank account.

The cheques for Rent and Advertising would be entered via 'Bank Payments'. Posting these will create Credit entries in the Bank account and Debit entries in the Rent and Advertising accounts.

The Cash Payments and Cash Receipts sections act in exactly the same way for cash transactions.

The Bank (or any other) Account can be viewed by selecting 'Account History' from the Nominal Ledger Reports menu. At the end of the month, it would be as it is shown here.

```
A/C Ref. : 0088                    A/C Name : Bank

No. Tp  Date    Ref     Details           Value      Debit     Credit
 1  BR  010187          Start up capital  8000.00   8000.00
 2  BP  020187  90001   Rent for Jan      1000.00              1000.00
 5  BP  210187  90002   Local Paper Ad      80.00                80.00
12  JD  210187  cash                      800.00     800.00
15  JD  300187  cash                     1000.00    1000.00
16  PP  300187  12345   Purchase Payments 1400.00              1400.00

                                         Totals  :  9800.00    2480.00
                                         Balance :  7320.00
```

43

Double-entry Bookkeeping – The Ledger System

Journal Entries

The transfer of money between Cash and Bank, or between any other two accounts must be done through journal entries. It is here that an understanding of the manual system helps most of all, for it is necessary to specify whether an amount is to be treated as a Debit or a Credit.

A payment of cash *into* the Bank needs entries to Credit Cash and Debit Bank; thus the journal entries to pay in £800 would be:

A/C No	(Account)	Date	Details	Debit	Credit
0088	Cash	210187	cash receipts		£800
0089	Bank	210187	cash receipts	£800	

Taking cash *from* the bank requires the reverse – Credit Bank and Debit Cash.

When equipment, furniture or whatever is bought on credit, the supplier – the Creditor – gets the Credit entry, and the account receiving the goods gets the Debit.

A/C No	(Account)	Date	Details	Debit	Credit
0066	Sundry Creditors	060187	Whitings Electrics		£200
0089	Cleaning	060187	Hoover	£200	

With another similar pair for the other credit purchase, Heather's entries to the accounts are complete for the month.

Double-entry Bookkeeping – The Ledger System

Palfreman Motor Spares

This is another small business, but here the accounts are slightly more complicated for two reasons; sales are a mixture of cash and credit, so customers' accounts are needed; goods sometimes prove to be faulty or are supplied in error – both to Palfreman and by him to customers – and the accounting system must be able to cope with returns.

Joe Palfreman started his business on March 1st. An accounting year can start at any time you like, though the first of a month is normal. Let's follow his first month's trading.

The Transactions
1. Mar 1st. Started up with £18,000 in the bank and £2,000 in cash.
2. Mar 3rd. Rented premises – paying in arrears – £200.
3. Mar 4th. Bought and paid for a security system – £400.
4. Mar 5th. Bought shelving and counter on credit – £600.
5. Mar 7th. Bought stock on credit – £8,000.
6. Mar 12th. Paid cash for a second-hand van – £1,000.
7. Mar 14th. Sales recorded – £400 cash, £300 and £700 on credit.
8. Mar 15th. Faulty goods returned to Palfreman... (£200).
9. Mar 16th. ... and by him to supplier. (£100)
10. Mar 19th. Phone connected at last – and paid for – £125.
11. Mar 20th. Bought keyrings to give to customers – £35.
12. Mar 22nd. More sales recorded – £700 cash. £1,100 on credit.
13. Mar 24th. Business trip to arrange dealership – £250.
14. Mar 28th. Wages paid – £200.
15. Mar 31st. Stock bought for cash – £1,500.

Double-entry Bookkeeping – The Ledger System

CAPITAL ACCOUNT

Date	Details	£	Date	Details	£
(1)			Mar 1	Bank	18,000
			Mar 1	Cash	2,000
				Balance	20,000

The starting capital has been split between Bank and Cash, and so requires two entries here as well as in the Cash Book. As long as the assets equal the capital, it does not matter how they are organised.

RENT ACCOUNT

Date	Details	£	Date	Details	£
(2) Mar 3	Russ Bros.	300			

RUSS BROS ACCOUNT

Date	Details	£	Date	Details	£
(2)			Mar 3	Rent	300

As the rent is paid in arrears, Russ Bros will be a creditor of the firm. It is therefore necessary to open up an account for them. There is a Debit entry under Rent, for Palfreman has gained an asset – his premises – and a Credit entry under Russ Bros.

Double-entry Bookkeeping – The Ledger System

SECURITY ACCOUNT

Date	Details	£	Date	Details	£
(3) Mar 4	Bank	400			

This is an essentially simple transaction, as the burglar alarm system was paid for by cheque immediately after installation. As it is quite likely that this will be the only purchase to fall under 'Security' in the foreseeable future, it is arguable that it is hardly worth a separate account. It could just as well have been included in the general Fixtures & Fittings account.

FIXTURES & FITTINGS ACCOUNT

Date	Details	£	Date	Details	£
(4) Mar 5	Fields	600			

FIELDS ACCOUNT

Date	Details	£	Date	Details	£
(4)			Mar 5	Fix & Fits	600

Palfreman has bought shelving and a counter unit to fit out his store, and as this was a credit purchase, has opened an account for the supplier. It is not always necessary to have an account for every credit purchase. If he was going to settle the debt within the same accounting period, and if there were to be no more purchases from this company, then it would be reasonable to delay the entry of the transaction into the accounts until the cheque was paid. It could then be treated as a cash purchase.

Double-entry Bookkeeping – The Ledger System

VAN ACCOUNT

Date	Details	£	Date	Details	£
(6) Mar 12	Cash	1,000			

A simple, if substantial, cash transaction, with a new account being created to handle this new asset. The actual name used for any account is a matter of personal choice – the only practical requirement is that it should be meaningful.

PURCHASES ACCOUNT

Date	Details	£	Date	Details	£
(5) Mar 7	Unibits	8,000			
(15) Mar 31	Cash	1,500			
	Balance	9,500			

UNIBITS ACCOUNT

Date	Details	£	Date	Details	£
(5)			Mar 7	Purchases	8,000
(9) Mar 15	Returns Outwd	100			
	Balance	7,900			
		8,000			8,000
				Balance c/d	7,900

RETURNS OUTWARDS ACCOUNT

Date	Details	£	Date	Details	£
(9)			Mar 15	Unibits	100

Two separate transactions are recorded in this set. First there is the purchase of stock on credit from Unibits, and this is entered in the normal way. Secondly, there is the return of faulty parts to the supplier. This is entered as a Debit in Unibits account – for the business has 'gained' in the sense that it has reduced its debt to the supplier; and as a Credit in

48

Double-entry Bookkeeping – The Ledger System

the Returns Outward account. Returned goods are better recorded in a separate account, rather than as a Credit entry in the Purchases Account. We will come back to returns when we look at Sales.

The end of the month accounting shows a total debt – Credit balance – to Unibits of £7,900. This is carried down into the next month.

SALES ACCOUNT

Date	Details	£	Date	Details	£
(7)			Mar 14	Cash	400
(7)			Mar 14	Thomas	300
(7)			Mar 14	Thurston Mtrs	700
(12)			Mar 22	Cash	700
(12)			Mar 22	Thurston Mtrs	1,100
				Balance	3,200

THOMAS ACCOUNT

Date	Details	£	Date	Details	£
(7) Mar 15	Sales	300			

THURSTON MOTORS ACCOUNT

Date	Details	£	Date	Details	£
(7) Mar 14	Sales	700			
(8)			Mar 15	Returns Inwd	200
(12) Mar 22	Sales	1,100		Balance	1,600
		1,800			1,800
	Balance c/d	1,600			

RETURNS INWARDS ACCOUNT

Date	Details	£	Date	Details	£
(8) Mar 15	Thurston Mtr	200			

Two sets of sales transactions are recorded here, from March 14th (7) and March 22nd (12). The cash sales will also be found as Debit entries in the Cash Book; and the credit sales can be seen as Debits in the two

49

Double-entry Bookkeeping — The Ledger System

customers' accounts. There has been one sale to Thomas, and the payment on that is still outstanding at the end of the month.

The situation with Thurston Motors is more complicated as a faulty part from the first batch was returned. This must be recorded as a Credit entry in the customer's account, and as a Debit in a special Returns Inwards Account. It cannot be simply debited from the Sales Account as this would imply that the part was available for resale. Being able to see at a glance the proportion of sales to returns is also a valuable aid to better management.

This is the part that we came across earlier being returned to the suppliers, Unibits. You should notice that it is here valued, correctly, at £200 though it appears as £100 where its return to the supplier is recorded. This reflects the sales mark-up.

TELEPHONE ACCOUNT

Date	Details	£	Date	Details	£
(10) Mar 19	Bank	125			

Telephone bills are inevitably a substantial expense for most businesses and merit their own account. The installation of March 19th is recorded by a Debit entry here and by a Credit entry in the Bank column of the Cash Book — it was paid for by cheque.

ADVERTISING ACCOUNT

Date	Details	£	Date	Details	£
(11) Mar 20	Cash	35			

This records the purchase of 100 keyrings embossed with 'Palfreman Motor Spares'. It is important to note that an Advertising Account is used, rather than one labelled 'Keyrings'. If a business buys products — keyrings, pens, calendars or whatever — to give away, then it does so for a reason. That reason is normally advertising, and the amount spent should be clearly recorded as advertising expenses.

Double-entry Bookkeeping – The Ledger System

TRAVEL ACCOUNT

Date	Details	£	Date	Details	£
(13) Mar 24	Bank	250			

Joe Palfreman's trip abroad to arrange a dealership in French auto spares was an essential business expense, and should therefore be recorded in a suitable expense account. If, however, it had been a pleasure trip to France, then the cost should have been written into his Drawings Account as it would have been a private expense. The owner of a business would normally draw out money, but could draw stock for private use, or even 'draw' a holiday.

WAGES ACCOUNT

Date	Details	£	Date	Details	£
(14) Mar 28	Cash	200			

The Wages Account is the last of the individual accounts that were brought into use during this first month of trading. Look for the corresponding Credit entry for this, and for the other expenses within the Cash Book.

CASH BOOK

Date	Debits	Cash £	Bank £	Date	Credits	Cash £	Bank £
(1) Mar 1	Capital	2,000	18,000				
(3)				Mar 4	Security		400
(6)				Mar 12	Van	1,000	
(7) Mar 14	Sales	400					
(10)				Mar 19	Telephone		125
(11)				Mar 20	Advertising	35	
(12) Mar 22	Sales	700					
(13)				Mar 24	Travel		250
(14)				Mar 28	Wages	200	
(15)				Mar 31	Purchases	1,500	
					Balance c/d	365	17,225
		3,100	18,000			3,100	18,000
	Balance b/d	365	17,225				

Double-entry Bookkeeping – The Ledger System

SUMMARY

- When goods are returned to a supplier, their value is recorded as a debit entry in the supplier's account and as a credit entry in an account marked *'Returns Outwards'* or *'Purchases Returns'*.

- When a customer returns goods – for whatever reason – this is a transaction to be recorded as a credit in the customer's account and a debit in *'Returns Inwards'* or *'Sales Returns'*.

- The accounts must make a clear distinction between the personal finances of the owner, and the finances of the business. Any goods or money taken from the firm for private use must be recorded under Drawings. Only costs that are incurred in the running or promotion of the business can be recorded as *expenses*.

The transfer to computer

By the end of March, Joe Palfreman had one credit supplier, two credit customers, and 17 other accounts. Allowing for expansion over the rest of the year, it would be reasonable to initialise for 50 Sales, 20 Purchases and 50 Nominal Accounts.

He will need these nominal accounts to handle this month's transactions.

0003 Furniture & Fittings	1000 Sales
0005 Van	(2) 1006 Returns Inwards
0035 Stock	1099 Discounts
0038 Debtors' Control	2001 Purchases
0065 Creditors' Control	(3) 2006 Returns Outwards
0066 Sundry Creditors	3001 Wages
(1) 0067 Russ Bros	3010 Rent
0069 Tax Control	3030 Telephone
0088 Cash	3120 Travel
0089 Bank	3140 Security
0095 Capital	3180 Advertising

1. Russ Bros could be handled under 'Sundry Creditors', but may be better kept separate. There are substantial sums involved, and all relate to the rent.

2. When goods are returned to Palfreman, he will record the transactions through the 'Sales Credit Notes' routine. Here he will give the references of the customer — so that a Credit can be entered in that account — and of the 'Returns Inwards' account where the debit entry will go.

3. Similarly, Returns Outwards will collect the credit entries when returns to a supplier are recorded through the **Purchase Credit Notes** routine.

Apart from the fact that many of the sales will be handled via the Sales Ledger, Palfreman's accounts are otherwise much the same as those of Heather's Café.

A partnership at work

Sole traders – one-man or one-woman businesses – form the majority of small businesses in the UK, but there are other types which must also be considered.

A partnership normally consists of between two and twenty people, each of whom has put capital into the venture. The capital does not have to be a set amount, nor does it have to be the same as that put in by other partners.

A partnership may be formed for different reasons. Two or more people who have worked together in the past, as employees of others, may decide to set up their own business. (And with so many works closures and cut-backs, redundancy money is a common source of capital.)

It may be that a person does not have all the capital that is needed to start the business, so the support of other interested parties must be found. These partners may take an active role in the firm, or, as 'sleeping partners' simply provide financial backing.

A husband and wife may form themselves into a partnership, even though one spouse may play only a limited role in the business. As partners, their tax position may be more favourable than it would be as sole trader and employee.

Among the many advantages of partnerships are that the extra resources of cash (and skills) can enable the business to grow faster and larger. Against that, the sole proprietor does have more freedom of action in that decisions can be taken without having to consult others – though it should be remembered that this also implies a greater freedom to make the wrong decisions!

The biggest drawback to partnerships is that each individual partner is liable to lose all his or her assets if the firm fails. There is no limit to this liability, so that – in theory at least – even a minor partner, with an initial investment of only a few thousand, could find his home at risk in the event of bankruptcy of the business.

Double-entry Bookkeeping – The Ledger System

Two-tone Cash And Carry

Messrs Black and White started their business at the beginning of 198– with £60,000 capital, several years of experience in distribution and high hopes for the future. They had made sure, before the outset, that they could get favourable credit terms from their main suppliers, and this sensible move helped them to get off to a good start.

Let's see how their accounts cope with that first month's trading.

The Transactions
1   Jan 1st. Black and White each put in £30,000 as starting capital.
2   Jan 4th. Paid £20,000 to the Building Society as a deposit on their new store (Cost £100,000).
3   Jan 6th. Paid £20,000 for refurbishments to the store.
4   Jan 9th. Obtained stock – £25,000, £40,000 and £15,000.
5   Jan 12th. Bought advertising space in the local paper – £350.
6   Jan 15th. A local celebrity is hired for the Grand Opening – £400
7   Jan 18th. Cash sales to date – £6,000.
8   Jan 20th. Insurance premium is paid – £2,400.
9   Jan 22nd. A surveyor is hired for the car park project – £600.
10 Jan 25th. Cash sales for the week – £30,000.
11 Jan 27th. Paid one of the suppliers for stock received at (4).
12 Jan 28th. Part payment to another supplier – £5,000.
13 Jan 29th. Large credit sale made – carriage cost £100.
14 Jan 30th. Further stock received, delivery charges of £150.
15 Jan 31st. After a good month, the entrepreneurs draw cash to celebrate – £200 each.

Two-Tone Cash and Carry
Accounts as at Jan 31st.

CAPITAL ACCOUNT

	Date	Details	£	Date	Details	£
(1)				Jan 1	Bank (Black)	30,000
				Jan 1	Bank (White)	30,000
					Balance	60,000

Only one Capital Account has been used, but the contributions of the two partners are clearly marked. It would have been equally possible to establish a separate Capital Account for each partner.

55

Double-entry Bookkeeping – The Ledger System

PREMISES ACCOUNT

Date	Details	£	Date	Details	£
(2) Jan 4	Building Soc	100,000			

BUILDING SOCIETY ACCOUNT

Date	Details	£	Date	Details	£
(2) Jan 4	Bank	20,000	Jan 4	Premises	100,000
	Balance	80,000			
		100,000			100,000
				Balance c/d	80,000

Two transactions are recorded here. The acquisition of the stores is first written in as an asset into the Premises Account and as a credit entry in the Building Society Account. The deposit of £20,000 also appears in this account and in the Cash Book.

In subsequent months, the mortgage repayments will be entered on the debit side, and interest charges will be written in as Credit entries at the end of each year. The value of the premises should be reassessed every year or so, especially as Two-Tone are in an area where property prices have been rising sharply.

FIXTURES & FITTINGS ACCOUNT

Date	Details	£	Date	Details	£
(3) Jan 6	Bank	20,000			

A simple entry here and in the Cash Book to record the payment by cheque for the redecoration and refitting.

PURCHASES ACCOUNT

Date	Details	£	Date	Details	£
(4) Jan 9	Allen	25,000			
Jan 9	Johnson	40,000			
Jan 9	Wimbourne	15,000			
(14) Jan 30	Wimbourne	6,000			
	Balance	86,000			

ALLEN ACCOUNT

Date	Details	£	Date	Details	£
(4) (11) Jan 27	Bank	25,000	Jan 9	Purchases	25,000

JOHNSON ACCOUNT

Date	Details	£	Date	Details	£
(4) (12) Jan 28	Cash	5,000	Jan 9	Purchases	40,000
	Balance	35,000			
		40,000			40,000
				Balance	35,000

WIMBOURNE ACCOUNT

Date	Details	£	Date	Details	£
(4)			Jan 9	Purchases	15,000
(14)			Jan 30	Purchases	6,000
					21,000

CARRIAGE INWARDS ACCOUNT

Date	Details	£	Date	Details	£
(14) Jan 30	Cash	150			

There's quite a lot going on here, so let's start on January 9th, when Black and White stock up on goods for their cash and carry. The transactions

Double-entry Bookkeeping – The Ledger System

are all credit purchases, and so appear in the Purchasess Account and in those of the individual suppliers.

Allen requires payment in full by the end of the month, but by that time enough money has come in from sales to pay the debt. If you look ahead to the Cash Book, you will see that on January 27th, Two-Tone pay £25,000 into the bank to cover a cheque for the same amount. This is recorded as a Cash to Bank, and as a Bank to Allen transaction. In a manual system, a short cut could be used here, recording a move from Cash to Allen and not bothering with the Bank entries. This is what is done with the £5,000 paid to Johnson.

The point to note with Wimbourne is that it is not related directly to the purchases. This firm offers free delivery on orders over £10,000, and the purchases of January 30th totalled less than this. Delivery charges of £150 were incurred. These are recorded in the separate Carriage Inwards account (and the Cash Book), and are not included in the normal Wimbourne account, which is only for purchases.

ADVERTISING ACCOUNT

Date	Details	£	Date	Details	£
(5) Jan 12	Bank	350			
(6) Jan 15	Bank (Opening)	400			
		750			

The cost of the full-page advert in the local paper was obviously to be entered in the Advertising Account, but the fee paid to the celebrity at the Grand Opening could arguably have been handled otherwise. As this was a fairly substantial sum, and an unusual expense, it could have merited an account of its own. Against that, a multiplicity of small accounts can cause a headache, and Two-Tone decided to treat it as an advertising expense.

INSURANCE ACCOUNT

Date	Details	£	Date	Details	£
(8) Jan 20	Bank	2,400			

No complications in the recording of this cheque for the Insurance Premium.

Double-entry Bookkeeping – The Ledger System

SPECIAL PROJECTS ACCOUNT

Date	Details	£	Date	Details	£
(9) Jan 22	Bank (Survey)	600			

Black and White are planning to make an extension to their car parking facilities. The first stage was to get a surveyor in to give them an estimate of the cost. This £600 represents his fee.

The partnership has other plans for the long-term development of their business, and the exploratory costs of these will also be included in their Special Projects Account.

SALES ACCOUNT

Date	Details	£	Date	Details	£
(7)			Jan 18	Cash	6,000
(10)			Jan 25	Cash	30,000
(13)			Jan 29	Dunks	8,000
					44,000

DUNKS LTD ACCOUNT

Date	Details	£	Date	Details	£
(13) Jan 29	Sales	8,000			

CARRIAGE OUTWARDS ACCOUNT

Date	Details	£	Date	Details	£
(13) Jan 29	Bank (Dunks)	100			

As befits a Cash and Carry, almost all of the sales are in cash or cheques – which are treated as cash while they are in the till. (Transactions (7) and (10).)

Their credit sale to Dunks raises the problem of delivery. As Two-Tone have no delivery van of their own, and outside contractor must be hired.

Double-entry Bookkeeping — The Ledger System

The cost is recorded in the Carriage Outwards Account, in the same way that the delivery of goods to Two-Tone was recorded in Carriage Inwards. Separate accounts are necessary for the two types of delivery cost as they are treated slightly differently as the overall accounting picture unfolds.

DRAWINGS (BLACK) ACCOUNT

Date	Details	£	Date	Details	£
(15)Jan 31	Bank	200			

DRAWINGS (WHITE) ACCOUNT

Date	Details	£	Date	Details	£
(15)Jan 31	Bank	200			

Note that while a single Capital Account was shared by the partners, each has his own Drawings Account. This is important, as each is liable to make a considerable number of drawings through the year and it would be difficult to separate them out from a single account.

Double-entry Bookkeeping – The Ledger System

CASH BOOK

Date	Debits	Cash £	Bank £	Date	Credits	Cash £	Bank £
(1) Jan 1	Capital(B)		30,000				
(1) Jan 1	Capital(W)		30,000				
(2)				Jan 4	Building Soc		20,000
(3)				Jan 6	Fix & Fits		20,000
(5)				Jan 12	Advertising		350
(6)				Jan 15	Advertising		400
(7) Jan 18	Sales	6,000					
(8)				Jan 20	Insurance		2,400
(9)				Jan 22	Special Proj		600
(10) Jan 25	Sales	30,000					
(11) Jan 27	Cash		25,000	Jan 27	Bank	25,000	
(11)				Jan 27	Allen		25,000
(12)				Jan 28	Johnson	5,000	
(13)				Jan 29	Carriage Out		100
(14)				Jan 30	Carriage In	150	
(15)				Jan 31	Drawings (B)		200
(15)				Jan 31	Drawings (W)		200
					Balance	5,850	15,750
		36,000	85,000			36,000	85,000
	Balance b/d	5,850	15,750				

The Cash Book entries have all been commented upon earlier as we have gone through the rest of the accounts. They are included here for completeness.

You will notice that the end of the month balancing shows that Two-Tone have taken £36,000 and paid out £30,150 in cash. A Debit balance of £5,850 is therefore carried over to the start of the next month. Similarly, in the Bank columns, the £85,000 debit and £69,250 credit totals leave a debit balance of £15,750.

61

Double-entry Bookkeeping – The Ledger System

SUMMARY

- In a partnership, each partner should have a separate *Drawings* account. A single Capital account will normally suffice, as there are likely to be few transactions recorded there over the course of a year.

- The category *'Advertising'* can comfortably encompass many activities undertaken to promote the firm.

- Where delivery charges need recording, there should be separate accounts for *Carriage Inwards and Outwards*.

The transfer to computer

A Mid-Year Start

This time we will explore what is needed to transfer from a manual system at some point during a financial year – in this case, at the end of the first month's trading.

We will start by going through the accounts, sorting them into type and noting the end of month balance on each. Reference names can then be allocated to the Purchase and Sales accounts, and reference numbers to the Nominal accounts.

1. The opening balance in the Debtors' Control account is the total of all money owed to the firm by credit customers.
2. Similarly, the Creditors' Control holds the total owed within the Purchase Ledger.
3. The Capital account has been split into two here, though it could have been left as a single entity with the partners' holdings noted in 'Details' written in the entries.

Double-entry Bookkeeping – The Ledger System

ACCOUNT	DEBIT	CREDIT	REFERENCE
Purchase Ledger			
Allen	-	-	ALLEN
Johnson		£3,500	JOHNS
Wimbourne		£2,100	WIMBO
Sales Ledger			
Dunks	£8,000		DUNKS
Nominal Ledger			
Fixed Assets			
Premises	£100,000		0001
Furniture & Fittings	£20,000		0003
Current Assets and Liabilities			
Stock	-	-	0035
(1) Debtors' Control	£8,000		0038
(2) Creditors' Control		£56,000	0065
Cash	£5,850		0088
Bank	£15,750		0089
Financing			
(3) Capital (Black)		£30,000	0095
Capital (White)		£30,000	0096
Building Society		£80,000	0097
Sales		£44,000	1000
Purchases	£86,000		2001
Carriage Inwards	£150		2007
Expenses			
Drawings (Black)	£200		3000
Drawings (White)	£200		3001
Insurance	£2,400		3090
Carriage Outwards	£100		3150
Advertising	£750		3180
Special Projects	£600		3240

The opening balances for the Nominal Accounts must be written in through the 'Journal Entries' routine. The others are handled through Ledger Postings in the Sales and Purchase Ledgers, as detailed in the User Manuals.

Once the accounts are set up and have their opening balances, future transactions can be recorded in the normal ways.

Double-entry Bookkeeping – The Ledger System

The Limited Company

Another alternative open to entrepreneurs is to form a limited company. Like a partnership this may involve as few as two individuals, but it has the advantage that the investors do not put their private possessions in jeopardy. Their liability for the debts of the firm is limited to the amount of their original investment. The most that any shareholder can lose is the money that was spent on buying shares in the company.

The law makes a distinction between a private and a public limited company; the main differences being that the public limited company requires a paid up share capital of at least £50,000 and must disclose certain information about its accounts. As we are only concerned with small businesses, the particular problems of public limited companies will be largely ignored in this book.

The shares in a limited company may be of several types:

- *Ordinary Shares.* With the most common type of share, the shareholders have voting rights, giving them a say in the running of the company. The dividend – the share of the profits – that they receive is not fixed, so these shares can give a handsome return if the firm is doing well. On the other hand, if the business does badly, the ordinary shareholders may see little or no return.

- *Preference Shares.* As the name implies, holders of this type of share get preferential treatment. Where there is only limited profit to distribute to shareholders, these will get their dividend first; and the owners of ordinary shares will have to make do with any residual profit.

Preference shares normally pay a fixed rate of return, say 5% on the face value of the share at the time of issue. Even if the business has an exceptional year, the preference shareholder will receive no more than this, though the ordinary shareholder may be enjoying a bumper dividend. In a poor year, even the preference shareholder will get a reduced return. What happens after that depends upon the nature of the share.

With a *Cumulative preference share,* any shortfall will be carried over, to be made up in subsequent years. Thus, if the share should have paid out £5 per £100, but the dividend had to be reduced to £3, the missing £2 will be made up in the first following year in which sufficient profit was available.

With a *non-cumulative preference share,* the shortfalls, if any, are not corrected in the future.

Grunks Ltd

Brandon Brannigan had been in the toy business, as a shop manager and as a sales rep, for a number of years. He had always wanted to set up on his own, on the manufacturing side, and when his daughter suggested the idea of a Grunk, he believed he had found a winner. Grunks — small furry figures of peculiar design — could well start a craze if properly marketed. He knew that if he wanted to make real money out of the idea he would have to manufacture them on a large scale and get them into the stores before any of the established toymakers could muscle in on the act. He also knew that it would take more capital than he had to start a factory.

Brannigan did his market research, drew up a business plan and trading forecast, and established Grunks Ltd. It had an authorised capital of £200,000 ordinary shares and £20,000 preference shares, though initially he only issued £160,000 ordinary and £10,000 preference shares. (The investors were those friends and relatives with faith in Grunks. Brannigan took the major shareholding using a private bank loan secured against his house.)

Grunks Ltd is a manufacturing firm, and therefore its accounts are somewhat different from those that we have looked at so far.

Double-entry Bookkeeping – The Ledger System

The Transactions
1 *Start-up date – Capital £160,000 + £10,000.*
2 *Jan 2nd. Bought up a small tailoring factory, complete with equipment, for £100,000.*
3 *Jan 3rd. Purchased raw materials from FunFur Fabrics – £12,000.*
4 *Jan 4th. Purchased a delivery van – £6,000.*
5 *Jan 12th. Sold first batch of grunks – £20,000.*
6 *Jan 14th. More materials from FunFur – £16,000.*
7 *Jan 16th. Cash sales to local store – £2,400.*
8 *Jan 18th. Repairs to van and fuel costs – £150 and £120.*
9 *Jan 21st. Commissions to sales reps – £1,200.*
10 *Jan 24th. Further share issue – £40,000.*
11 *Jan 27th. Payment on credit sale, and some returns – £2,000.*
12 *Jan 28th. Staff wages – £800.*
13 *Jan 30th. More credit sales – £21,000.*
14 *Jan 31st. Directors' fees paid – £400.*
15 *Jan 31st. Electricity bill paid – £60.*

Double-entry Bookkeeping – The Ledger System

ORDINARY SHARE CAPITAL ACCOUNT

	Details	£	Date	Details	£
(1)			Jan 1	Bank	160,000
(10)			Jan 24	Bank	40,000
					200,000

PREFERENCE SHARE CAPITAL ACCOUNT

Date	Details	£	Date	Details	£
(1)			Jan 1	Bank	10,000

The business has raised its capital through the issue of two types of shares, and it is important that each should have its own account. The 7% Cumulative Preference Shares pays a dividend of – as you might guess – 7%, or 7p per annum for every £1 share.

EQUIPMENT ACCOUNT

Date	Details	£	Date	Details	£
(2) Jan 2	Bank	20,000			

FACTORY PREMISES ACCOUNT

Date	Details	£	Date	Details	£
(2) Jan 2	Bank	80,000			

Although the factory and its equipment were bought through a single transaction, the two elements must be recorded in separate accounts. It was estimated that the sewing machines and other items of equipment were worth £20,000, and the premises £80,000. As we saw with Two-Tone, the value of the premises should be reassessed annually; and Grunks will need to open another account at some point to handle the depreciation on their equipment. We will return to depreciation when we look at Sue's Salon.

Double-entry Bookkeeping – The Ledger System

PURCHASES ACCOUNT

Date	Details	£	Date	Details	£
(3) Jan 3	FunFur	12,000			
(6) Jan 14	FunFur	16,000			
	Balance	28,000			

FUNFUR FABRICS ACCOUNT

Date	Details	£	Date	Details	£
(3)			Jan 3	Purchases	12,000
(6)			Jan 14	Purchases	16,000
				Balance	28,000

For the retailer, distributor and wholesaler, 'Purchases' refer to stocks of ready-made goods. The manufacturer handles raw materials under this category. It is the same in all cases, in the sense that these are the items upon which the business will make its profits.

MOTOR VEHICLES ACCOUNT

Date	Details	£	Date	Details	£
(4) Jan 4	Bank	6,000			

MOTOR REPAIRS ACCOUNT

Date	Details	£	Date	Details	£
(8) Jan 18	Bank	150			

MOTOR EXPENSES ACCOUNT

Date	Details	£	Date	Details	£
(8) Jan 18	Bank (Fuel)	120			

Notice here that vehicles (initially only the van) and their running expenses are handled by three different accounts. The van itself is an asset. If running costs were debited from the Motor Vehicle Account, this would imply an increase in the value of the asset – which would be highly

Double-entry Bookkeeping – The Ledger System

misleading. Repairs and fuel costs could be included in the same account, but are best kept separate if only because, at present, fuel is zero-rated for VAT, while the repairs are taxed at standard rate. Separate accounts also give better information on costs. If running costs are high, is it because the van has reached the stage where it is uneconomical to continue to repair it, or is it because fuel is being used on private mileage?

SALES ACCOUNT

Date	Details	£	Date	Details	£
(5)			Jan 12	SuperToys	20,000
(7)			Jan 16	Cash	2,400
(13)			Jan 30	SuperToys	21,000
				Balance	43,400

SUPERTOYS ACCOUNT

Date	Details	£	Date	Details	£
(5) Jan 12	Sales	20,000			
(11)			Jan 27	Bank	18,000
(11)			Jan 27	Sales Returns	2,000
(13) Jan 30	Sales	21,000		Balance	21,000
		41,000			41,000
	Balance	21,000			

SALES RETURNS ACCOUNT

Date	Details	£	Date	Details	£
(11) Jan 27	SuperToys	2,000			

COMMISSIONS PAYABLE ACCOUNT

Date	Details	£	Date	Details	£
(9) Jan 21	Bank	1 200			

The first batch of Grunks were supplied to SuperToys on January 12th. After trial marketing in two of their stores, SuperToys have decided that two of the variations on the basic Grunk design are not likely to sell in large quantities, and returned these on January 27th. Though disappointed, Brannigan was willing to oblige this important customer by accepting the returns. This transaction is recorded in the SuperToys

Double-entry Bookkeeping – The Ledger System

and Sales Returns Accounts. The rest of the range have been well received, and SuperToys have ordered more of these for their other stores.

Notice also that commissions payable to the sales rep are recorded in a special account. They represent an expense to the business and are written as a Debit entry here. They will also be seen on the Credit side of the Cash Book.

WAGES ACCOUNT

Date	Details	£	Date	Details	£
(12) Jan 28	Bank	800			

DIRECTORS' FEES ACCOUNT

Date	Details	£	Date	Details	£
(14) Jan 31	Bank	400			

Although directors' fees are similar to wages, they have a different position within the business, are subject to different constraints, and must be handled separately.

ELECTRICITY ACCOUNT

Date	Details	£	Date	Details	£
(15) Jan 31	Bank	60			

The premises are all electric – for heat, light and power. While it would be useful to be able to split the costs between the factory and the office, this is not practicable without installing separate meters.

Double-entry Bookkeeping – The Ledger System

CASH BOOK

Date	Debits	Cash £	Bank £	Date	Credits	Cash £	Bank £
(1) Jan 1	OS.Capital		160,000				
(1) Jan 1	PS.Capital		10,000				
(2)				Jan 2	Equipment		20,000
(2)				Jan 2	Factory Prem		80,000
(4)				Jan 4	Motor Vehicle		6,000
(7) Jan 16	Sales	2,400					
(8)				Jan 18	Motor Repair		150
(8)				Jan 18	Motor Expense		120
(9)				Jan 21	Commissions		1,200
(10) Jan 24	OS.Capital		40,000				
(11) Jan 27	SuperToys		18,000				
(12)				Jan 28	Wages		800
(14)				Jan 31	Directors		400
(15)				Jan 31	Electricity		60
					Balance	2,400	119,270
		2,400	228,000			2,400	228,000
		======	=======			======	=======
	Balance	2,400	119,270				

SUMMARY

■ In a limited company, the capital is raised through the issue of shares. The return on an *Ordinary Share* depends entirely on the profitability of the company, and how much it retains for future investment. Holders of *Preference Shares* have first claim on the profits of a company, but receive a restricted dividend.

■ An asset, and the costs of maintaining that asset, are treated in separate accounts. This is as true of motor vehicles and their running costs, and of premises and their maintenance as it is of any other asset.

■ The distinction between personal and business finances must be even sharper here than in the case of a sole trader or partnership. (Even though the individual running the company may own 99% of the shares.) There can be no 'Drawings' account. Any money paid by the business to its 'owners' must be in the form of dividends, directors' fees or salaries.

Double-entry Bookkeeping – The Ledger System

The transfer to computer

As a manufacturing firm and a limited company, Grunks Ltd will need an accounting structure that differs in some key areas from any of those that we have seen so far. Initialisation will follow the same course – setting up for 50 accounts in the Purchase Ledger, 100 in Sales and 100 in Nominal; and the Nominal Accounts listed below would be sufficient to handle all the transactions to date. However – as you will see further on in the book – new accounts will be needed to cope with the costing of production and the allocation of profit.

0001 Premises
0003 Equipment
0005 Motor Vehicles
0035 Stock – Raw Materials
0038 Debtors' Control
0065 Creditors' Control
0069 Tax Control
0088 Cash
0089 Bank
0095 Ordinary Share Capital
0096 Preference Share Capital

1000 Sales
1006 Sales Returns
1099 Discount

2001 Purchases
2500 Commission
2510 Labour
3000 Directors' Fees
3110 Motor Repairs
3112 Petrol
3170 Electricity

Double-entry Bookkeeping – The Ledger System

Small is beautiful

In this last of our examples, we will be looking at ways of handling two other key areas of accounting – discounts and depreciation – in the context of a firm in the service sector. The most noticeable change in these accounts are the discount columns in the Cash Book. This is the *Three-Column Cash Book*. It is in common use, though many businesses find that they can manage perfectly well with the Two-Column version that we have used up to this point.

Sue's beauty salon

When Sue started up in business, she did so as a limited company rather than as a sole trader or in partnership with her husband. There were a number of reasons for this. She wanted to have solid foundations for later expansion; she believed the business would quickly grow to the point where there were tax advantages in this arrangement; and the capital behind the venture was to come from her and her husband's joint savings. He was not going to be able to take an active part in the business, though they both felt it fair that he should have a (small) shareholding in it.

The Transactions
1. *Aug 1st. Sets up business with £5,000 ordinary share capital.*
2. *Aug 4th. Purchase equipment on credit – £3,000.*
3. *Aug 5th. Buys stock to use in salon – £400.*
4. *Aug 6th. Buys cleaning materials – £60.*
5. *Aug 12th. First week's receipts – £120.*
6. *Aug 14th. Buys stock on credit – £70.*
7. *Aug 17th. Pays for equipment and gets discount of £300.*
8. *Aug 19th. Week's cash receipts – £400.*
9. *Aug 21st. ABC (local company) arrange for employees to use Sue's salon on credit basis – discount agreed (£200).*
10. *Aug 22nd. Bank loans Sue £2,000 to buy sunbeds.*
11. *Aug 26th. Week's cash receipts – £220.*
12. *Aug 28th. Wages paid in cash. Sue takes her salary of £300.*
13. *Aug 30th. ABC settle monthly bill – £180.*
14. *Aug 30th. Accountant advises Sue to write depreciation into her accounts – £60 equipment, £40 sunbeds.*
15. *Aug 31st. Vist to trade show – £6 ticket and expenses.*

Double-entry Bookkeeping – The Ledger System

ORDINARY SHARE CAPITAL ACCOUNT

Date	Details	£	Date	Details	£
(1)			Aug 1	Bank	4,000
(1)			Aug 1	Cash	1,000
					5,000

Sue decides to retain £1,000 of her capital in cash to meet the early costs of the business. The remainder is paid into the firm's bank account.

EQUIPMENT ACCOUNT

Date	Details	£	Date	Details	£
(2) Aug 4	ACI	3,000			
(14)			Aug 30	Depreciation	60
				Balance	2,940
		3,000			3,000
	Balance	2,940			

ACI LTD ACCOUNT

Date	Details	£	Date	Details	£
(2)			Aug 4	Equipment	3,000
(7) Aug 17	Bank	2,700			
(7) Aug 17	Disc. Rec'd	300			
		3,000			3,000

DEPRECIATION OF EQUIPMENT ACCOUNT

Date	Details	£	Date	Details	£
(14) Aug 30	Equipment	60			

The credit purchase of equipment follows the normal pattern – credit supplier's account, debit Equipment. It is what happens next that is of more interest to us. ACI offered a 10% discount for settlement within fourteen days, and Sue made sure that she paid in time to get this. The discount is entered, along with the payment, as a debit entry in the supplier's account – this brings both sides into balance. Its equivalent credit entry is written in the discount column on the credit side of the Cash Book. (In a computerised system, this would be handled via a special Discount account.)

Double-entry Bookkeeping – The Ledger System

Secondly, when Sue was going over her books with her accountant at the end of the month, he recommended that depreciation of the equipment should be written in from the start. This is not simply a reflection of the declining value of the equipment, but a recognition that it has a limited life-span and will need replacing at some time. Sue estimates that after four years it will all need replacing, and that its residual value will be effectively zero. By writing in depreciation at £60 per month, its cost will be spread over that time.

Sue could have waited until the end of the year and then written in £720 to cover the period. Depreciation is more usually recorded on an annual basis.

Notice how depreciation is handled through a debit entry in a separate account, and a credit entry under Equipment. The net value of the Equipment (on the Debit side) is therefore reduced, but the total debits remain the same.

PURCHASES ACCOUNT

	Date	Details	£	Date	Details	£
(3)	Aug 5	Cash	400			
(6)	Aug 14	Pipper	70			
		Balance	470			

PIPPER ACCOUNT

	Date	Details	£	Date	Details	£
(6)				Aug 14	Purchases	70

CLEANING MATERIALS ACCOUNT

	Date	Details	£	Date	Details	£
(4)	Aug 6	Cash	60			

The 'stock' that Sue buys (and records under Purchases) is not for resale directly, but it is an essential component in the services that her salon provides. Like the manufacturer's raw materials, these items are central to profit-making.

Cleaning materials are not immediately related to the beautician

Double-entry Bookkeeping – The Ledger System

services, and are instead recorded as an expense on the business. They could equally well be entered under the General Expenses heading. In exactly the same way, her receipts from customers are recorded as Sales, even though no actual goods change hands.

SALES ACCOUNT

Date	Details	£	Date	Details	£
(5)			Aug 9	Cash	120
(8)			Aug 20	Cash	400
(9)			Aug 21	ABC	200
(11)			Aug 24	Cash	220
				Balance	940

ABC LTD ACCOUNT

Date	Details	£	Date	Details	£
(9) Aug 21	Sales	200			
(12)			Aug 26	Bank	180
(12)			Aug 26	Disc. Allowed	20
		200			200

Most of Sue's business is from cash customers – the salon does, after all, provide a personal service to individuals – but she was very happy to make the arrangement with ABC for its employees. In return for a steady level of business, worth around £200 per month, the salon has agreed a 10% discount, with the bill settled by a single cheque at the end of the month. Discount Allowed is treated as a mirror image of Discount Received. It appears as a credit in the customer's account, and in the discount column on the credit side of the Cash Book.

WAGES ACCOUNT

Date	Details	£	Date	Details	£
(13) Aug 28	Cash	200			

SALARY ACCOUNT

Date	Details	£	Date	Details	£
(14) Aug 31	Bank	300			

Double-entry Bookkeeping – The Ledger System

As always, staff wages and owners' or directors' remuneration are handled by separate accounts.

BANK LOAN ACCOUNT

Date	Details	£	Date	Details	£
(10)			Aug 22	Bank	2,000

SUNBEDS ACCOUNT

Date	Details	£	Date	Details	£
(10) Aug 22 (14)	Bank	2,000	Aug 30	Depreciation Balance	40 1,960
		2,000 ========			2,000 ========
	Balance	1,960			

DEPRECIATION OF SUNBEDS ACCOUNT

Date	Details	£	Date	Details	£
(14) Aug 30	Sunbeds	40			

Within a few days of opening her Salon, Sue realised that she really needed to be able to offer the use of sunbeds to her customers – and that this could be a useful source of extra income. She negotiated a loan of £2,000 from the bank, and bought her sunbeds on August 22nd. The transaction was recorded in two stages – Bank Loan Account to Bank, then Bank to Sunbeds Account. The shortcut – Credit Bank Loan, Credit Sunbeds – could have been used instead.

Notice also that Sue has set up a depreciation account for the sunbeds. They are to be written off over three years, at £40 per month. This will leave a residual value of around £500, their estimated second-hand value at that time.

Double-entry Bookkeeping — The Ledger System

GENERAL EXPENSES ACCOUNT

Date	Details	£	Date	Details	£
(15) Aug 31	Cash	6			

This records the cost of going to a trade show — a typical small expense that is best handled under a global account like this.

CASH BOOK

Date	Debits	Disc.	Cash £	Bank £	Date	Credits	Disc.	Cash £	Bank £
		All'd					Rec'd		
(1) Aug 1	Capital		1,000	4,000					
(3)					Aug 5	Purchases		400	
(4)					Aug 6	Cleaning		60	
(5) Aug 9	Sales		120						
(7)					Aug 17	ACI	300		2,700
(8) Aug 20	Sales		400						
(10) Aug 22	Bank Loan			2,000	Jan 22	Sunbeds			2,000
(11) Aug 24	Sales		220						
(12) Aug 26	ABC	20		180					
(13)					Aug 28	Wages		200	
(13)					Aug 28	Salary		300	
(15)					Aug 31	Gen Exp.		6	
						Balance		774	1,480
		20	1,740	6,180			300	1,740	6,180
	Balance	20	774	1,480		Balance	300		

The extra columns — Discount Allowed and Discount Received — are often simply headed 'Discount' in manual Cash Book pages. You should notice that there is no attempt to balance out the two discount columns. Each total is carried on separately to the next month. As you will see in the next section, these discounts are brought into play when drawing up a Trial Balance and the Balance Sheet.

Double-entry Bookkeeping — The Ledger System

SUMMARY

- A limited company can be as small as a sole trader operation. It does not need to have a capital base of tens of thousands, or a turnover in the six-figure range.

- Almost all equipment will lose its value over time, or need to be replaced sooner or later. Its depreciation should therefore be assessed and written into the accounts. This can be done equally well on a monthly or annual basis.

- A bank loan needs to be recorded via a separate account — it cannot be simply incorporated into the normal 'Bank Account'.

The transfer to computer

For the most part, these accounts will pose no more problems than any of the first three in the set. Sue should initialise for around 10 Sales, 10 Purchase and 50 Nominal accounts; and the first of these to be set up should include the following:

0003 Equipment	(1) 0004 Depreciation — Equipment
0005 Sunbeds	(1) 0006 Depreciation — Sunbeds
(2) 0030 Discount	0035 Stock
0038 Debtors' Control	0065 Creditors' Control
0066 Sundry Creditors	0069 Tax Control
0088 Cash	0089 Bank
0095 Ordinary Share Capital	0097 Bank Loan
1000 Sales	(2) 1099 Discount — Trading
2001 Purchases	3000 Directors' Salaries
3001 Wages	3080 Cleaning
3210 Sundry Expenses	

1 Depreciation is handled via separate accounts, as with a manual system. It is marked off against equipment by Journal Entries; e.g. Debit Equipment £60, Credit Depreciation £60. Journal Entries are slower to manage than any other in the system, simple because two entries are required for each transaction. Therefore — unless there is an overriding need for monthly depreciation — this might perhaps be done on an annual basis.

Double-entry Bookkeeping – The Ledger System

2. Notice that there are two accounts for Discount. The first of these (0030) is for discounts on equipment and expenses – i.e. non-resale purchases. Any discounts received here must be recorded via the Journal Entries routine, with a Credit for the Discount and a Debit for the other account. The second (1099) will handle those given on Sales and received on Purchases. No special entries are required to record these, as the Sales Receipts and Purchase Payments routines have a Discount option. By numbering the account as 1099, it can be pulled in with the Sales accounts (1000 to 1099) or with the Purchase accounts (1099 to 2499) when setting the layout of accounts for the Trading, Profit and Loss Accounts. Trading discounts must be kept separate from other ones as they affect the Gross and Nett Profit calculations differently – as you will see in later sections.

3

End of Period Accounts

The Trial Balance

You have seen that at the end of each month, each account has been 'balanced off'; that is, the entries on the two sides have been totalled, and where the totals are not the same, the Debit or Credit balance has been carried over to the start of the next accounting period. These balances form the raw data for the Trial balance.

Throughout the section on double-entry bookkeeping, we have emphasised the fact that every transaction must be recorded twice – once as a Debit and once as a Credit. (Though, as you have seen, with Sage accountancy software, the user will generally only need to make one entry. The other will be made by the program.) The main purpose of the Trial Balance is to check that entries have been made properly.

In the Trial Balance, all of the Debit and Credit balances are totalled and compared. The sums on the two sides should be the same. If there is a discrepancy it will indicate that a transaction has only been recorded once, or that one of the values was entered wrongly – the value may have been changed, or the entry put in the wrong column. Now with a Sage package these errors simply will not happen during normal operation.

The value that is entered for a transaction will be automatically posted to two accounts – once as a credit and once as a debit – and it will be the same in both. If a discrepancy does show up in the Trial Balance here, it will be because the data disk has been corrupted or because the program was interrupted in the middle of an operation – perhaps through power failure or operator error.

There are other errors that will not show up in the Trial Balance. A transaction could have been missed out completely. An entry could have been posted to the wrong account – though to the right side. Thus if 'Debit Jones £50' was entered as 'Debit Gladstone £50' the balance would be unaffected, though Jones would not be happy. A number may be mis-read – e.g. £67 instead of £76 – but if the same value is used for both entries, the totals will still balance.

There is no infallible way of preventing these errors from creeping in, though they can be minimised by a well-organised data collection system and by double checking at entry time. Once they are there, you can only find them by working back through the account books, or the Audit Trail and Account Histories in a Sage package, comparing the entries in the accounts with the original invoices or other documents.

There are probably as many opportunities for making these kinds of errors in a computer system as there are in a manual one. However, the saving grace of the computer system is that the whole process of doing the accounts is much less arduous and less time-consuming. The operator is less likely to make mistakes through tiredness or loss of concentration, and will have more time for checking the entries.

So, treat the Trial Balance as no more than the first line of defence against error. The only guarantee that it gives is that if it balances, then every transaction has been recorded as a debit and as a credit.

Let's turn now to our sample businesses and look at their Trial Balances. You will find it useful to compare them with the firms' accounts shown in the last section. Remember that not all of the individual accounts are included in a Trial Balance. The only ones that are used are those where there was a credit or debit balance at the end of the accounting period.

In the Trial Balance, the debit balances are listed in the column marked 'Dr', and credit balances under the heading 'Cr'. For simplicity, we have grouped them into two distinct sets, but in practice, accounts may appear in any order. Those people and companies to whom the business owes

End of Period Accounts

money may be listed individually, as they are here, or grouped into a single entry labelled 'Sundry Creditors'. Similarly, those owing money to the business may be grouped under 'Sundry Debtors', or listed in full.

In a computerised system, the totals owing or owed in the Sales and Purchase Ledgers will be shown under Debtors' Control and Creditors' Control. In other respects, the Trial Balance — selected from the Nominal Ledger Reports menu — is the same as in a manual system. It can be called up at any time, and is therefore a useful way of checking that Journal Entries have been done the right way. (It is very easy, when you are just starting to do your own accounts, to confuse Debit and Credit!)

Heather's Cafe Trial balance as at 31st January

		Dr £	Cr £
	Cash	315	
	Bank	7,170	
	Rent	1,000	
	Fixtures & Fittings	2,000	
	Purchases	3,100	
	Advertising	80	
	Cleaning	200	
	Wages	80	
	General Expenses	10	
	Drawings	120	
	Capital		8,000
(Creditors)	Roberts		2,000
	Davies		1,700
	Whiting		200
	Sales		2,175
		28,075	28,075

Notice that the Trial Balance tells you nothing about the profitability of the business, though the final figures give some indication of its scale.

83

End of Period Accounts

Palfreman Motor Spares   Trial balance as at 31st March

		Dr £	Cr £
	Cash	365	
	Bank	17,225	
	Rent	300	
	Security	400	
	Fixtures & Fittings	600	
	Purchases	9,500	
	Van	1,000	
(Debtors)	Thomas	300	
	Thurston Motors	1,600	
	Telephone	125	
	Advertising	35	
	Travel	250	
	Wages	200	
	Returns Inwards	200	
	Capital		20,000
(Creditors)	Russ Bros		300
	Fields		600
	Unibits		7,900
	Sales		3,200
	Returns Outwards		100
		32,100	32,100

Two-tone Cash & Carry   Trial balance as at 31st January

	Dr £	Cr £
Cash	5,850	
Bank	15,750	
Premises	100,000	
Fixtures & Fittings	20,000	
Purchases	86,000	
Debtors' Control	8,000	
Insurance	2,400	
Advertising	750	
Special Projects	600	
Carriage Outwards	100	
Carriage Inwards	150	
Drawings (Black)	200	
Drawings (White)	200	
Capital		60,000
Building Society		80,000
Creditors' Control		56,000
Sales		44,000
	240,000	240,000

In this Trial Balance you should notice that individual debtors' and creditors' accounts have been replaced by the Control accounts which show the total sums involved. This is how they will appear in most manual three-ledger systems, and in Sage accountancy software.

Grunks Ltd   Trial balance as at 31st January

	Dr £	Cr £
Cash	2,400	
Bank	119,270	
Equipment	20,000	
Premises	80,000	
Purchases	28,000	
Motor Vehicles	6,000	
Motor Repairs	150	
Motor Expenses	120	
Debtors' Control	21,000	
Electricity	60	
Sales Returns	2,000	
Wages	800	
Commissions Payable	1,200	
Directors' Fees	400	
Ordinary Share Capital		200,000
Preference Share Capital		10,000
Creditors' Control		28,000
Sales		43,400
	281,400	281,400

End of Period Accounts

Sue's Beauty Salon Trial balance as at 31st August

		Dr £	Cr £
	Discount Allowed	20	
	Cash	774	
	Bank	1,480	
	Equipment	2,940	
	Purchases	470	
	Cleaning Materials	60	
	Sunbeds	1,960	
	Wages	200	
	Drawings	300	
	Depreciation of Equipment	60	
	Depreciation of Sunbeds	40	
	General Expenses	6	
	Discount Received		300
	Ordinary Share Capital		5,000
	Bank Loan		2,000
(Creditor)	Pipper		70
	Sales		940
		8,310	8,310

Note that Discount Allowed is entered on the Debit side of the Cash Book, and thus appears in the Debit column here; likewise Discount Received is written in the Credits. In the Sage account systems, all Sales and Purchase discounts would be normally brought together in the Trading Discount account, while those relating to expenses would be handled by a separate Expenses Discount.

Equipment and Sunbeds and the Depreciation of each have all been allocated separate accounts here, but in practice all categories of similar equipment would normally be handled by one account, and all depreciation by a second.

SUMMARY

- The Trial Balance draws together all the end of period balances from the individual accounts, totalling all Debits and Credits.

- Any discrepancy between these totals will indicate an error (or errors) somewhere in the accounts.

- The Trial Balance only acts as a check on the double entries. Errors that affect both sides equally will not show up.

- The Trial Balance says nothing about the profitability or otherwise of a business.

End of Period Accounts

Manufacturing Accounts

After the Trial Balance has been constructed, the next stage for most firms is to pull together the Trading Accounts. However, those firms in the business of making goods, rather than buying and selling them, must first draw up a Manufacturing Account. The main purpose of this exercise is to find the cost of producing the goods that they have sold. The production cost figure will then be used in the Trading and Profit and Loss Account in place of the 'Purchases' value that non-manufacturing firms would use.

In a manual bookkeeping system, the Manufacturing Account is split into several sections. The first section involves the direct costs — those costs that are central to the process of manufacturing the products. The usual direct costs include raw materials, labour (on the shopfloor but not in the offices), royalties paid to inventors or patent-holders, and direct expenses such as the power used in the factory and the cost of hiring equipment to complete a specific job.

The sum total of those costs is usually referred to as the *Prime Cost* of production.

```
  RAW MATERIALS
  FACTORY LABOUR
+ DIRECT EXPENSES
  ROYALTIES
  _____
= PRIME COST
```

The Prime Cost therefore represents the total of those expenses which can be identified as being directly attributable to the manufacture of units of production, as opposed to the general costs incurred within the factory. A key feature of these costs is that they will vary in relation to the levels of production. The more you make, the more raw materials you need.

There are other manufacturing costs which will remain more or less constant, however many products are made. The rent is the same whether the firm manufactures 20 or 20,000 widgets a week. These costs that are related to production, but not directly attributable to any actual units of production, are usually grouped under the heading 'Factory Overhead Expenses'.

End of Period Accounts

```
  RAW MATERIALS
  FACTORY LABOUR
+ DIRECT EXPENSES
  ROYALTIES
  ─────────────────
  PRIME COST
+ FACTORY OVERHEADS
  ─────────────────
= FACTORY COST
  ─────────────────
```

Taken together, the Prime Cost and the Factory Overheads give a total Factory Cost. There is one more adjustment that must be made before we have a final figure to tell us how much it cost, in all, to produce however many units were manufactured. Few manufacturing processes are so simple that a product is either finished or not. There are almost always intermediate stages of 'completeness' — even Grunks pass through six stages: sew parts, stuff, sew together, add features, dress and box. The value of part-finished goods at the start and at the end of the trading year must be taken into account.

To make this adjustment, we must add in the value of 'Work in Progress' at the start of the year, and deduct the value of it at the end. In effect, the production costs of part-made products is carried over into the year in which they will be completed and sold.

```
  RAW MATERIALS
  FACTORY LABOUR
+ DIRECT EXPENSES
  ROYALTIES
  ──────────────────────────────
  PRIME COST
+ FACTORY OVERHEADS
  ──────────────────────────────
  FACTORY COST
+ WORK IN PROGRESS (1st Jan.)
− WORK IN PROGRESS (31st Dec.)
  ──────────────────────────────
  PRODUCTION COST OF COMPLETED GOODS
  ──────────────────────────────
```

We are now in a position to be able to work through a complete manufacturing account for a typical small firm.

End of Period Accounts

Manufacturing Account for the Year Ending 31st December 198-

		£	£
(1a)	Opening Stock of Raw Materials		400
	Add Purchases		14,000
(2)	Add Carriage Inwards		200
			14,600
(1b)	Less Closing Stock of Raw Materials		300
(3)	Cost of Raw Materials Consumed		14,300
	Direct Wages		5,400
	Direct Expenses		600
	PRIME COST		20,000
	Factory Overhead Expenses		
	Heat & Light	1,000	
(4)	Indirect Wages	2,000	
	Servicing of Equipment	500	
	Depreciation	400	
(5)	Factory Rent & Rates	2,500	
	Factory Insurance	450	
	General Factory Expenses	150	7,000
	FACTORY COST		27,000
	Add Work in Progress 1st Jan.		5,000
			32,000
	Less Work in Progress 31st Dec.		2,000
	PRODUCTION COST OF GOODS COMPLETED		30,000

Notes

- It is the cost of the raw materials that have been used, rather than the cost of those that were bought during the year, that is important. The expression 'Old Stock + Purchases − Current Stock' gives us that figure.

- Carriage Inwards. In the earlier section on double-entry book-keeping, we noted that delivery charges should be split into Carriage Inwards and Outwards. The charge that a supplier makes for delivery is equivalent to an extra cost on the purchase, and must be added onto that for accounting purposes. On a personal level, it is the same

End of Period Accounts

with mail order buying. The stated price of an article may be low, but when you add on post and packing, wouldn't it be cheaper to go to the shops?

- The true cost of raw materials is therefore cost of materials used, plus carriage inwards.

- Indirect wages are those that are not directly attributable to production, for example, those of cleaners and maintenance staff.

- Where rent is paid in a single transaction for the whole premises, it must be apportioned between factory and office for this exercise. Similarly, so must rates, heat and light, security and any other shared costs.

Only Grunks Ltd, among our example business, are manufacturers, and there is little to be gained from drawing up a manufacturing account based on their first month's figures. At that stage, they haven't incurred enough different costs to give a realistic picture. However, if we project the business forward and allow them to trade for a year, we will have a more meaningful situation.

We will start with the Trial Balance as it might appear at the end of the year. There are some extra accounts, and some of those that were listed individually in the earlier balance have been grouped together here, so that we can keep the focus on the manufacturing aspects of the accounts.

End of Period Accounts

Grunks Ltd

Trial balance as at 31st December

	Dr £	Cr £
Ordinary Share Capital		200,000
Preference Share Capital		10,000
Cash	11,000	
Bank	47,000	
Equipment	20,000	
Premises	80,000	
Wages (Direct)	185,000	
(Indirect)	25,000	
(Administration)	15,000	
Purchases	125,000	
Sales		425,000
Creditors		50,000
Debtors	34,500	
Carriage Inwards	4,000	
Factory Indirect Expenses	91,000	
Directors' Fees	15,000	
Commissions Payable	12,000	
Discounts Allowed	7,500	
Rates	8,000	
Office Expenses	5,000	
	685,000	685,000

The other figures that we will need before we can draw up the manufacturing account are the year-end work in progress and stock valuations. (As this is a new business, there are no start of year figures for these.) These values cannot be found from the accounts but must be assessed within the factory. It is important that valuations are done on a consistent basis if a true picture is to emerge.

As you can see, not all of the information in the Trial Balance is used in the Manufacturing Account opposite. But it must be remembered that this is only concerned with one – albeit crucial – aspect of the business, and it should be seen as only one of the stages through which an accountant will work in order to arrive at a final set of accounts.

End of Period Accounts

Grunks Ltd.
Manufacturing Account for the year ending 31st December 198-

	£	£
Opening Stock of Raw Materials		-
Add Purchases		125,000
Add Carriage Inwards		4,000
		129,000
Less Closing Stock of Raw Materials		6,200
Cost of Raw Materials Consumed		122,800
Direct Wages		185,000
PRIME COST		307,800
Factory Overhead Expenses		
Indirect Wages	25,000	
Factory Indirect Expenses	91,000	116,000
FACTORY COST		423,800
Add Work in Progress 1st Jan.		–
		423,800
Less Work in Progress 31st Dec.		35,000
PRODUCTION COST OF GOODS COMPLETED		388,800

SUMMARY

■ The purpose of the Manufacturing Account is to find the cost of producing the firm's goods. This value will be needed in drawing up the Trading Account.

■ Manufacturing costs are divided into two sections.
Direct Costs are attributable directly to the manufacture of goods and will depend upon production levels. *Indirect Costs* are related to the overall running of the factory.

■ Work in Progress and stocks of raw materials and part-finished goods must be taken into account.

End of Period Accounts

Using the Sage Accountancy Systems

While it is not possible to produce a properly laid out Manufacturing Account (i.e. as a single document) within the Sage accountancy systems; there is no difficulty in performing all the necessary calculations. The results can be drawn from the system and typed up for presentation, and the key figure – that of Production Cost – can be incorporated into the Trading and Profit and Loss account.

There are essentially two ways of performing the Manufacturing Account calculations within the Sage systems. The first follows the manual system very closely, setting up accounts for Raw Materials, Prime, Factory and Production Cost and working through the calculations stage by stage. This has the advantage of producing the intermediate costings in a clear readable form – something that may be useful for later analysis and cost control. The second method is a short cut and only gives the final Production Cost.

Whichever method you choose, you must start by assessing the value of the stock of raw materials and of work in progress. You will then need to create nominal accounts to hold this information. You will also need an account for Production Cost of goods completed, and – if you want the intermediate figures – for the Raw Materials, Prime and Factory Costs. Ideally, these should all be located in the Purchases area of the Nominal Ledger. If Grunks Ltd was using Accountant or Financial Controller, then this part of the Trading Account would look like this:

 2000 Opening Stock (Raw Mat's)   2001 Purchases
 2006 Purchase Returns   2007 Carriage Inwards
 2010 Closing Stock (Raw Mat's)   2012 RAW MATERIALS
 2020 PRIME COST   2030 FACTORY COST
 2035 Work in Progress   2040 PRODUCTION COST
 2500 Commissions Payable   2510 Direct Wages
 2520 Factory Indirect Expenses   2530 Indirect Wages

The Manufacturing Account is produced entirely by Journal Entries. The sequence needed is shown below. (Figures as in the manual example.)

1   Credit Purchases £6,200   Debit Closing Stock £6,200

This takes the Purchases down from £125,000 to £118,800.

End of Period Accounts

2   Credit Purchases   £118,800   Debit Raw Materials £118,800
    Credit Carriage Inwards £4,000   Debit Raw Materials   £4,000

Any Opening Stock value should also be carried across in the same way. All of the costs are thus transferred, and totalled, into the Raw Materials account.

3   Credit Raw Materials £122,800   Debit Prime Cost   £122,800
    Credit Direct Wages £185,000   Debit Prime Cost   £185,000

This clears the Raw Material and Direct Wages accounts, and leaves a total of £307,800 in the Prime Cost account.

4   Credit Prime Cost   £307,800   Debit Factory Cost   £307,800
    Credit Factory Indirect £91,000   Debit Factory Cost   £91,000
    Credit Wages Indirect   £25,000   Debit Factory Cost   £25,000

Again, costs are accumulated into the next account in the chain. This gives a Factory Cost figure of £423,800.

5   Credit Factory Cost   £35,000   Debit Work In Progress £35,000

The asset — part finished goods — is removed, so that the Factory Cost is now £388,800

6   Credit Factory Cost   £388,800   Debit Production Cost £388,800

... and the final figure is transferred to the Production Cost account.

At the end of this process, the Trial Balance will show Debit balances in Production Cost, Closing Stock (Raw Materials) and Work In Progress. All other accounts in this area will have been cleared; the intermediate costs can always be seen by looking through the Account Histories.

The Short Cut
If you do not need to have the Raw Materials, Prime and Factory Costs as separate figures, then some of these Journal Entries can be omitted. After the Closing Stock (Raw Materials) value has been deducted from Purchases and Carriage Inwards added, the resulting Purchases figure can be transferred with all other direct and indirect costs into the Production Cost account. Work In Progress should then be deducted from that. The final Production Cost balance will be exactly the same as in the longer method, but none of the intermediate costings are recorded.

End of Period Accounts

The sequence is then:

1 Credit Purchases £6,200   Debit Closing Stock £6,200

2 Credit Carriage Inwards £4,000   Debit Purchases £4,000

3 Credit Opening Stock £.....   Debit Purchases £.....

4 Credit Purchases £122,800   Debit Production Cost £122,800
   Credit Direct Wages £185,000   Debit Production Cost £185,000
   Credit Factory Indirect £91,000 Debit Production Cost £91,000
   Credit Wages Indirect £25,000   Debit Production Cost £25,000

5 Credit Production Cost £35,000   Debit Work In Progress £35,000

The Trading Account

Note that the 'Bookkeeper' package does not offer a Trading Account or Balance sheet facility. It is assumed that the user will be presenting the Trial Balance, Audit Trail and other reports to an accountant for the final analysis.

After the accuracy of the accounts has been checked by the Trial Balance, and — in the case of manufacturers only — the Manufacturing Account has been drawn up so that the production costs are known, then it is possible to begin to assess the profitability of a business.

The first stage in this is the construction of a Trading Account. In essence, this compares the cost of goods sold with the income from sales, to find the Trading or Gross Profit — or Loss. The cost of goods sold is calculated in much the same way as the cost of raw materials in a Manufacturing Account. Take the start of year value of stock, add in the purchases and deduct the end of year stock figure. Any carriage charges and commissions due to salesmen should also be included in this cost of goods sum.

In a manual system, the Trading Account is an account just like any other. It is part of the double-entry system, with a debit and credit side. The main difference is that it is a summary account, drawing its information from elsewhere in the system.

End of Period Accounts

In the Sage accountancy systems, the Trading Account does not have a separate existence, but is organised as a section within the Nominal Ledger.

Sales, Purchases and any accounts dealing with returns and direct expenses should all be located there. The software can then calculate the Gross Profit on demand at any point during or at the end of the year. It is therefore very simple to keep a monthly or quarterly check on the performance of the business.

A simple (manual) Trading Account takes this form:

Trading Account for the year ending 31st December 198-

```
                            £                      £
Opening Stock           1,000       Sales      20,000
Add Purchases          15,000
                       ──────
Less Closing Stock      2,000
                       ──────
Cost of Goods Sold     14,000
GROSS PROFIT            6,000
                       ──────                  ──────
                       20,000                  20,000
                       ══════                  ══════
```

As with a manufacturing account, the stock valuations cannot be derived from the Trial Balance or the individual accounts, but must be assessed separately. Valuation of stock must also be done on a consistent basis — and there are several alternatives here which we will examine later in the chapter on Stock Control.

'*Stock*' means stock of goods ready for sale — so that in a manufacturing firm it is the value of finished goods that is used here, and not that of raw materials.

'*Purchases*' refers only to goods bought for resale. Purchases of equipment, vehicles, buildings and the like are not included — unless the firm trades in equipment, vehicles or buildings. A manufacturing company will use the production cost of finished goods in place of 'Purchases'.

The Purchases and Sales figures should include all transactions, whether cash or credit. It is the profitability of trading which is at issue here, not how much is owing to whom.

End of Period Accounts

In the example, there has been some stock-building during the year, so that the cost of goods sold is less than that of purchases. Simple arithmetic shows us that this firm made £6,000 Gross Profit from sales of £20,000. It must be remembered that this is Gross Profit and that the running costs of the business must be deducted to arrive at the final Nett Profit. We will return to this in the next section.

We can now hang a few refinements or to this basic framework. The true cost of goods and value of sales will normally be affected by returns and other charges.

Trading Account for the year ending 31st December 198-

```
                          £        £                         £        £
Opening Stock                   1,000   Sales           20,000
Add Purchases        15,000             Less Sales Returns  250   19,750
Less Purchase Returns   500    14,500
Add Carriage Inwards              300
                               ──────
                               15,800
Less Closing Stock              2,000
                               ──────
Cost of Goods Sold             13,800
GROSS PROFIT                    5,950
                               ──────
                               19,750                            19,750
                               ══════                            ══════
```

Note that Returns Outwards are deducted from Purchases. As the goods were returned to the supplier, they were not actually bought. Similarly, Returns Inwards must be deducted from the Sales figure.

Commissions to salesmen and Carriage Inwards charges — both of which are directly related to the quantity of goods sold — will increase the cost of goods, and must be added to the Purchases value.

In this example, we have total Sales of £19,750, being £20,000 less returns of £250. Take the Cost of Goods Sold from this, and we have a Gross Profit of £5,950.

Time now to turn to our five firms and look at their Trading Accounts. The first month's trading that we saw in the earlier section is not sufficient for this, so we will move on and take the figures from the end of their first and second years.

The object here is not simply to work out the Gross Profits, but also to

End of Period Accounts

use those figures to assess the progress of the businesses. This is, after all, what accounting is all about. It's not just number-crunching and keeping records for the taxman. A good set of accounts can be an invaluable aid to the better management of a business.

Heather's Café

Trading Account as at December 31st (Year 1)

	£		£
(1) Opening Stock	–	(2) Sales	88,000
(2) Add Purchases	60,000		
(3) Less Closing Stock	5,000		
Cost of Goods Sold	55,000		
(4) GROSS PROFIT	33,000		
	88,000		88,000

1. As this was the first year of trading, there was no opening stock.
2. Figures extracted from the Trial Balance.
3. Closing Stock valued at cost price.
4. A healthy Gross Profit, but the running costs of the business have to be subtracted before we can see the real profitability.

Trading Account as at December 31st (Year 2)

	£	£		£	£
Opening Stock		5,000	Sales	89,000	
Add Purchases	64,000		Less Sales Returns	100	88,900
Less Purchase Returns	1,000	63,000			
Add Carriage Inwards		50			
		68,050			
Less Closing Stock		3,100			
Cost of Goods Sold		64,950			
GROSS PROFIT		23,950			
		88,900			88,900

In this year's Trading Account, we have brought in the real-life complications of returns and carriage costs. We can also include an Opening Stock figure, which you will note is – of course – the same as the previous year's Closing Stock.

End of Period Accounts

The Purchases Returns here were probably unsuitable deliveries of foodstuffs, while the Sales Returns relate to dissatisfied customers. Fortunately, there do not seem to have been many of them, but Heather appears to be having some difficulties with her suppliers.

You will notice that the Gross Profit is substantially down on the previous year. Heather would do well to investigate the reasons for this as soon as possible.

Palfreman Motor Spares

In the first year of business, Joe Palfreman made a Gross Profit of £43,000 on Sales of £116,000. We will pass over the details of that first Trading Account and go direct to the end of his second year.

We will take the information that we need from the Trial Balance and the stock ledger.

Extracted Trial Balance as at December 31st (Year 2)

	£	£
Sales Returns	5,000	
Purchases Returns		4,500
Carriage Inwards	1,750	
Purchases	91,000	
Sales		117,000

Stock Ledger
Opening Stock (1st Jan) £11,000
Closing Stock (31st Dec) £30,000

Trading Account as at December 31st (Year 2)

	£	£		£	£
Opening Stock		11,000	Sales	117,000	
Add Purchases	91,000		Less Sales Returns	5,000	112,000
Less Purchase Returns	4,500	86,500			
Add Carriage Inwards		1,750			
		99,250			
Less Closing Stock		30,000			
Cost of Goods Sold		69,250			
GROSS PROFIT		42,750			
		112,000			112,000

End of Period Accounts

The Gross Profit, though very reasonable for a business of this size, is virtually the same as the previous year and this may give cause for concern. Ideally, profits should increase – particularly over the first few years of a business's life. This is a time for establishing a place in the market and building up a body of regular customers.

Two-tone Cash & Carry

In their first year of business, Two-Tone made a Gross Profit of £102,000 on turnover of £504,000. If their bank account felt a bit slim at the end of the year, it was because much of this profit was absorbed by stock-building. This left them in a good position at the start of the second year. We will focus on that. The figures, as always, are extracted from the Trial Balance and the stock books.

Trading Account as at December 31st (Year 2)

	£	£		£	£
Opening Stock		75,000	Sales	630,000	
Add Purchases	510,000		Less Sales Returns	8,000	622,000
Less Purchase Returns	15,000	495,500			
Add Carriage Inwards		6,000			
		576,000			
Less Closing Stock		95,000			
Cost of Goods Sold		481,000			
GROSS PROFIT		141,000			
		622,000			622,000

A quick glance over the Trading Account shows that Two-Tone's Gross Profit has risen to £141,000 – an increase over the previous year of around 40%. Look a little closer, and you will note that the Sales have risen from £504,000 to £622,000 – an increase of just under 22%. If we were able to talk to Messrs Black and White, we would probably find that, having established their customer base, they have not had to offer so many special discounts in their second year; and have thus been able to improve their margins by a few percent.

End of Period Accounts

Grunks Ltd

We will take both of the Trading Accounts in full this time, as they raise a number of interesting points.

Trading Account as at December 31st (Year 1)

	£	£		£	£
Opening Stock		-	Sales	425,000	
Add Production Cost			Less Sales Returns	38,000	387,000
of Goods Completed		388,800			
Add Commissions Payable		14,000			
		402,800			
Less Closing Stock		32,000			
Cost of Goods Sold		370,800			
GROSS PROFIT		16,200			
		387,000			387,000

Grunks Ltd's first year was not a resounding success. A Gross Profit of £16,200 on a turnover of £387,000 is not very good for a manufacturing firm — especially one in the 'craze' business. No matter how popular Grunks are, they cannot be expected to remain in fashion for long. Brannigan had underestimated the manufacturing costs of the toys, and overestimated the price he would be able to get from the dealers.

Trading Account as at December 31st (Year 2)

	£	£		£	£
Opening Stock		32,000	Sales	604,000	
Add Production Cost			Less Sales Returns	7,000	597,000
of Goods Completed		525,500			
Add Commissions Payable		6,500			
		564,000			
Less Closing Stock		28,000			
Cost of Goods Sold		536,000			
GROSS PROFIT		61,000			
		597,000			597,000

Comparing the two years, we will see that Sales have risen by around 40%, and while Production Costs have also gone up, they have done so less sharply. The problem of the high level of Sales Returns seems to have been brought under control, and it would appear that Grunks have made a substantial reduction in the commission rates to the salesmen. The result of all this is a much improved Gross Profit. However, we must remember that there are other expenses to be taken into account. We shall return to these later.

Sue's Salon

Trading Account as at December 31st (Year 1)

	£	£		£	£
Opening Stock		-	Sales	12,250	
Add Purchases	3,140		Less Sales Returns	50	12,200
Less Purchase Returns	40	3,100			
		3,100			
Less Closing Stock		200			
Cost of Goods Sold		2,900			
GROSS PROFIT		9,300			
		12,200			12,200

Sue's Salon would appear to have a very high profit margin on sales, but this is a service sector business, not a retail firm. The 'stock' used in the beauty treatment is only a small component of the cost. Wages and indirect expenses can be expected to be relatively high in this kind of firm. The overall profitability of the firm may therefore not be as good as it might appear at first sight.

SUMMARY

- The Trading Account draws together information from those other accounts relating to trading profits.

- Gross Profit is calculated by subtracting the cost of purchases and of direct expenses from the sale value of those goods.

- Accurate end of year stock valuations are essential.

- There is a section labelled 'Trading Account' in the Nominal Ledger of the Sage systems. Sales, Purchase and other direct expense accounts are located there. As Trading and Profit and Loss Accounts are handled within a single routine, we shall wait until the end of the next section before seeing how they work.

End of Period Accounts

The Profit and Loss Account

The Profit and Loss Account goes on from the Trading Account to consider the overheads and other indirect expenses incurred by the business, and their effect on the overall profit. Other forms of income will also be included in these calculations – rent from property, bank interest, dividends from shares owned by the firm.

Nett Profit = Gross Profit + Other Income – Indirect Expenses.

It is from this Nett Profit that the business must find its cash for future growth, for the sole trader's personal income or – in a company – the shareholders' dividends.

The types of accounts that will appear in the Profit and Loss Account include:

Office Sundries	Light & Heat
Salaries	Insurance
Directors' Fees	Maintenance
Depreciation	Motor Vehicle Expenses
Cleaning	Carriage Outwards
Postage	Stationery
Discounts Allowed	Discounts Received
Bank Charges	Bank Interest
Rent & Rates	Rent Received

The Profit and Loss Account of a small business may be no more complex than this:

Profit & Loss Account for the year ending 31st September 198-

	£		£
Wages	2,000	Gross Profit	10,000
Motor Expenses	1,500		
Insurance	200		
Electricity	1,100		
Depreciation - Cars	1,000		
- F & F	500		
Nett Profit	3,700		
	10,000		10,000

It is worth noting that the expenses of a business are not always directly related to the cash flow during the accounting period. Depreciation is the prime example here. You may spend £4,000 on a computer installation, but only its depreciation — say £800 — will be taken into account in determining that year's Nett Profit. The remaining £3,200 must be accounted for elsewhere. In subsequent years, the depreciation on this equipment will continue to eat into the firm's profit.

Profit & Loss Account for the year ending 31st December 198-

		£			£
	Wages	3,500		Gross Profit	10,000
	Motor Expenses	900	(1)	Discounts Received	500
	Rent & Rates	2,200	(2)	Bank Interest	250
(1)	Discounts Allowed	300			
	Insurance	200			
	Postage	120			
	Electricity	600			
	Depreciation - Cars	1,500			
	- F & F	750			
	General Expenses	1,000	(3)	Nett Loss	350
		11,070			11,070

1. Discounts Allowed — those given by the business to its customers — count as an expense and are charged as such in the Profit and Loss Account. Similarly, Discounts Received should be considered as non-sales income, and included here rather than in the Trading Account.

2. Bank Interest is clearly non-trading income.

3. Unfortunately, not every business makes a profit! In some sectors a Nett Loss in the early years may be almost inevitable. High start-up costs and the long lead-times in developing products or building a customer base will always cause initial problems.

Let's see how our five businesses are doing.

End of Period Accounts

Heather's Café

Profit & Loss Account for the year ending 31st December 198-

	£		£
Wages	12,000	Gross Profit	33,000
Cleaning Costs	1,500		
Insurance	450		
Decorating	335		
Disposable Items	400		
General Expenses	150		
Nett Profit	18,165		
	33,000		33,000

Here we see that the £33,000 trading profit has been cut to almost half by the costs incurred in making that profit. In this business, as in most others, the wage bill is the single greatest expense. As such, it is an area which should always be closely monitored.

Two-tone Cash & Carry

On a larger scale, we will see the same kind of picture with Two-Tone. There, almost 60% of the Gross Profit is taken up by the running costs, but there still remains a Nett Profit of over £40,000 for the partnership.

Profit & Loss Account for the year ending 31st December 198-

	£		£
Wages	45,000	Gross Profit	102,000
Maintenance	1,500		
Insurance	2,400		
Advertising	1,500		
Rates	3,000		
Overalls	1,000		
Heat & Light	2,000		
General Expenses	3,100		
Nett Profit	42,500		
	102,000		102,000

Grunks Ltd

The position here is less happy, as you can see. The Gross Profit was not impressive, given the turnover, and is more than outweighed by the firm's expenses.

Profit & Loss Account for the year ending 31st December 198-

	£		£
Wages (Admin)	15,000	Gross Profit	16,200
Directors' Fees	15,000		
Sales Commissions	12,000		
Discounts Allowed	7,500		
Rates	8,000		
General Expenses	5,000	Nett Loss	46,300
	62,500		62,500

There may seem to be relatively few expenses listed in this account, but it must be recalled that many of them were included in the earlier manufacturing account.

One might well argue that the directors scarcely merit their fees of £15,000 given that the business has shown a substantial Nett Loss!

Sue's Salon

When we looked at the Trading Account of Sue's Salon, we saw a Gross Profit of over £9,000 on sales of just over £12,000. We noted then that this was a poor guide to overall profitability because of the high level of other expenses — principally labour — in this, as in other, service industries. The Profit and Loss Account confirms these reservations about the business.

Profit & Loss Account for the year ending 31st July 198-

	£		£
Wages	4,000	Gross Profit	9,300
Cleaning	400		
Depreciation	1,200		
Telephone	110		
Rent & Rates	1,600		
Repairs	120		
Stationery	60		
Nett Profit	1,810		
	9,300		9,300

End of Period Accounts

Palfreman Motor Spares

For the sake of clarity, we have treated the Trading and Profit and Loss Accounts as separate entities, but in practice they are normally combined into a single statement. In this last example, we will view Palfreman's accounts in full, working up from the Trial Balance through to the Nett Profit.

Extracts from the Trial Balance as at 31st December (Year 1)

	£	£
Purchases	84,000	
Sales		116,000
Wages	16,000	
Insurance	600	
Depreciation - van	400	
Repairs to Windows	500	
Stationery	150	
Postage	50	
Discount Allowed	200	
General Expenses	1,000	

Note: Stock as at 31st December — £11,000

End of Period Accounts

Trading, Profit & Loss Account for the year ending 31st December 198-

	£	£		£	£
Opening Stock		-	Sales	121,000	
Add Purchases	86,500		Less Sales Returns	5,000	116,000
Less Purchase Returns	3,000	83,500			
Add Carriage Inwards		500			
		84,000			
Less Closing Stock		11,000			
Cost of Goods Sold		73,000			
GROSS PROFIT		43,000			
		116,000			116,000
Wages		16,000	Gross Profit		43,000
Rent & Rates		3,800			
Insurance		600			
Depreciation - Van		400			
Repairs to Window		500			
Stationery		150			
Postage		50			
Discounts Allowed		200			
General Expenses		1,000			
Nett Profit		20,300			
		43,000			43,000

The overall picture is much the same as that of Heather's Cafe or Two-Tone Cash & Carry, with around half of the Gross Profit being absorbed by the expenses of the business.

The Trading And Profit And Loss Accounts in the Sage Accountancy System

The system is designed to perform all Profit calculations for you, but some preparation is needed before it can do this. The Nominal Accounts should have been set up so that all sales-related ones are numbered from 1000, purchase-related from 2000, direct costs from 2500 and indirect costs from 3000. The Closing Stock of goods for resale (or Finished Goods) should be assessed, and its value deducted from Purchases (or from Production Cost in a manufacturing business) and transferred to the Closing Stock account.

End of Period Accounts

Select through the menus 'Management Reports' and 'Monthly Accounts' to reach 'Profit & Loss'. You will be asked to specify the range of accounts to include under the headings Sales, Purchases, Direct Costs and Overheads. When the profit is calculated, it will be done by totalling the balances in each set then working out the sums:

GROSSPROFIT = SALES − PURCHASES − DIRECT COSTS

NETT PROFIT = GROSS PROFIT − OVERHEADS

Sales should be straightforward. All the accounts from 1000 to 1099 − Sales of different lines, returns and discounts − need to be totalled to give a final Sales figure. Any Debit balances, in Sales Returns or Discount, are deducted from the total.

Purchases are a little trickier as stock needs to be taken into account. Opening Stock, all categories of Purchases, and Purchase Returns should be included in the range specified for the Profit and Loss calculations. Closing Stock should *not* be included. This is carried over to appear as the Opening Stock at the next end of period.

For the manufacturer, the 'Purchases' set should include Opening Stock of Finished Goods and Production Cost only. All other costs will have been absorbed within the Manufacturing Account calculations.

The Direct Costs and Overheads categories should pose no problems as long as you have not included any asset accounts within the expenses ranges.

Once ranges have been set, you can get the Trading and Profit and Loss Account by selecting Accounts Printout.

End Of Period Adjustments

In the Trading and Profit and Loss Accounts described in the last two sections we have deliberately simplified the accounting picture. In practice there are a number of complications which may arise.

One problem is that expenses entered into the accounts may not relate to the period in question. A business may well be paying in arrears for some things, and in advance for others. In accounting, these payments are called *accruals* and *prepayments*.

End of Period Accounts

Items may be omitted from the double-entry system during the course of the year. When they are discovered, they have to join the end of the year accounts. There may be other accounts to adjust in the light of reality – when does a debt become a bad debt?

Accruals

Accruals are monies owing in respect of expenses. Rent, rates, electricity and telephone bills are commonly paid in arrears – to a greater or lesser extent.

Consider a business which has its year ending on 31st December and which pays its telephone bills quarterly. Even if it pays promptly on receipt of the bill, there are still likely to be monies outstanding at the end of the year if only because the bills are made up at the end of the charge period. For example:

	£	
1st Quarter	200	4th April
2nd Quarter	220	5th July
3rd Quarter	240	2nd October
4th Quarter	210	6th January

The last payment will not have occurred before the end of the financial year, and so there will be an accrual of £210. If we translate this into the terms of double-entry bookkeeping, we will see this:

TELEPHONE ACCOUNT

Date	Details	£	Date	Details	£
Apr 3	Bank	200	Dec 31	Profit & Loss	870
Jul 5	Bank	220			
Oct 2	Bank	240			
Dec 31	Owing	210			
		870			870
				Owing	210

You will note that the Profit and Loss Account has been charged with £870, made up of the £660 which was paid, and the £210 owing. Within the Telephone Account, the £210 will be carried forward into the next year as a credit balance. The debt has not actually been paid, but the bill has been included as an expense in the year that it was incurred.

End of Period Accounts

Prepayments

These are mirror images of accruals, in that they are expenses paid in advance of the time to which they relate. Rent may be paid in advance; insurance almost always is.

Take this example of a business paying £300 a quarter for insurance. The first premium was paid as the contract was taken out, shortly after the start of the year. Thereafter, premiums are due – and paid – before the start of each quarter.

	£	
1st Quarter	300	5th January
2nd Quarter	300	31st March
3rd Quarter	300	30th June
4th Quarter	300	28th September
1st Quarter (Year 2)	300	29th December

The records of these transactions can be seen in the Insurance Account. Notice that only £1,200 – the year's premiums – are passed to the Profit and Loss Account. The last £300 is marked as Pre-Paid, and will be carried over to the start of the next year as a Debit balance.

INSURANCE ACCOUNT

Date	Details	£	Date	Details	£
Jan 5	Bank	300	Dec 31	Profit & Loss	1,200
Mar 31	Bank	300		Pre-Paid	300
Jun 30	Bank	300			
Sep 28	Bank	300			
Dec 29	Bank	300			
		1,500			1,500
	Balance	300			

Notes On The Accounts

The problems raised by accruals and prepayments will be met, and dealt with, while completing the set of accounts, but there may be other items that come to light after the Trial balance has been drawn up. Stock valuations, bad debts, over- and under-payments are all examples of

End of Period Accounts

these, and it is possible to bypass the main double-entry system when dealing with these. The transactions can be added as Notes to the summary accounts. Each must be entered twice – and for once this applies to a computerised as well as to a manual system. One Note will be entered in the Manufacturing, Trading, or Profit and Loss Account (as appropriate); the second in the Balance sheet – an aspect of the accounts that we shall turn to shortly.

We shall work through a full Trading and Profit and Loss Account to see how these things all fit together.

Trading, Profit & Loss Account for the year ending 31st December 198-

		£	£		£	£
	Opening Stock		10,000	Sales	100,000	
	Add Purchases	50,000		Less Sales Returns	1,000	99,000
	Less Purchase Returns	700	49,300			
	Add Carriage Inwards		500			
			59,800			
(1)	Less Closing Stock		14,000			
	Cost of Goods Sold		45,800			
	GROSS PROFIT		53,200			
			99,000			99,000
	Rent	6,000		Gross Profit		53,200
(2)	Less Pre-Paid	800	5,200	(3) Profit from Van Sale		300
	Salaries & Wages		14,000	Discounts Received		650
	General Expenses		1,500	Rent from Sublet	350	
	Electricity		2,300	(4) Accrued	350	700
	Insurance	600				
(5)	Accrued	300	900			
	Depreciation :					
	Equipment		1,100			
	Motor Vans	1,500				
(6)	Over-depreciation	200	1,300			
	Bad Debts		100			
(7)	Provision for Bad Debts		1,100			
	Vehicle Running Costs	200				
(8)	Accrued	400	600			
	Discounts Allowed		400			
	Nett Profit		26,350			
			54,850			54,850

End of Period Accounts

1. Closing Stock does not appear in the Trial Balance. It is written as a Note in the Trading Acccount, and in the Balance Sheet. As elsewhere in the double-entry system, each transaction must be recorded as both a debit and a credit.
2. The rent bill of £6,000 was an over-statement as £5,200 should have been paid. The additional £800 is treated as a prepayment and written in here, and in the Balance Sheet.
3. This firm does not trade in motor vehicles. When it made a profit of £300 on the sale of a van, this was not dealt with in the Trading Account, but had to be entered here, in the Profit and Loss Account.
4. The premises rented by the business are too large for its immediate needs, and a part has been sublet to a small firm at a rent of £700 a year, payable 6-monthly in arrears. £350 is outstanding at the end of the accounting year.
5. The accrual here is an overdue insurance premium of £300 that relates to that year's cover.
6. The over-depreciation of a motor van is a common occurrence. Here, the van had been depreciated at its usual rate, but was then sold before the end of the year. Thus the business was depreciating a van that it did not own. The problem is solved by reducing the amount of the depreciation in the Profit and Loss Account (and showing this in the Balance Sheet). Here the adjustment of £200 reduces the chargeable depreciation to £1,300.

    The opposite can also happen. In this example, the firm might have replaced its old van with a new one – that would have to be depreciated at a faster rate. if this is not written into the normal accounts, the additional expense could be written in here.
7. The Bad Debt is one that the firm knows will never be paid – the debtor has disappeared.

    Provision for Bad Debts is slightly different. The assumption here is that there will always be some bills that are not paid for one reason or another. No matter how trustworthy your customers, their ability to pay is not always entirely in their control.

    Bankruptcies do occur, and they can have a knock-on effect, with the failure of one business bringing down its weaker creditors. It is normal to write in a *Provision for Bad Debts* at around 2% of the total debtors' figure – though in high-risk businesses the cautious manager will set aside rather more for bad debts.

End of Period Accounts

Adjustments in a Computerised System

The key here is in the use of the Journal Entries routine, for this is the main way in which money is transferred between accounts. Before performing these end of period adjustments, you must create Nominal Accounts for Prepayments – in the Current Assets area – and for Accruals – in the Current Liabilities area. Bad Debts and Provision for Bad Debts accounts (though the two can be treated as one) will also be needed – in the Profit and Loss area, for these are Indirect Expenses against profit.

Accruals are Credit balances, so to record an underpayment of £300 on the Insurance account, the journal entries would be:

Debit Insurance £300   Credit Accruals £300

Prepayments are Debit balances. Thus, to mark £800 of the rent as being prepaid, you would need these journal entries:

Credit Rent £800   Debit Prepayments £800

Bad Debts are also Debit items. How these are treated will depend upon whether they are actual debts from bankrupt customers, or merely provision for such. Provision is handled by transferring monies from the Debtors' Control account, with the 'Details' field recording the nature of the transaction. So, if Debtors' Control stood at £10,000 and the firm was allowing 2%, the end of the year entries would be:

Credit Debtors' Control £200   Debit Bad Debts £200

Where a customer has gone out of business, the debt needs to be removed from the Sales Ledger, as well as from Debtors' Control. This can be done by using the Sales Credit Notes routine, specifying the Bad Debts account for the debit entry – rather than the Sales Returns account which would take the debit for a normal Credit Note. As the Debtors' Control account is simply the sum of all customers' balances, removing the debt from the customer's account also removes it from Debtors' Control.

As the debt would probably have been anticipated to some extent in the Provision for Bad Debts, the figure for this should be adjusted afterwards.

End of Period Accounts

Appropriation Accounts

The purpose of an appropriation account is to split up monies between the partners or shareholders in a business. The two situations are different in a number of respects and must be considered separately.

Partnerships

A partnership, as we noted earlier, can consist of anything between two and twenty people. If there are more potential 'partners' than that, then it is normally necessary to form the business into a limited company instead.

People can enter into a partnership without any formal written agreement, but it is much wiser to have a solicitor draw up a document setting out the financial arrangements before the business starts to operate. Disputes over money are all too common – and partnerships are very largely about money.

There are several aspects to the accounts that need to be agreed upon:

- The capital to be contributed by each partner.
- The ratio in which profits (or losses) are to be shared.
- The rate of interest to be paid on capital.
- The rate of interest to be charged on drawings.
- The partners' salaries.

1. Capital is rarely constant over time. The initial investments will rise and fall as partners leave in the business those payments that accrue to them, or withdraw money for other purposes. A separate capital account for each partner is the simplest solution.

2. The Partnership Act of 1890 states that unless the partners have a written agreement to the contrary, any profits or losses shall be shared equally by all. Where partners have contributed different amounts of capital, or give varying amounts of their time to the business, then this simple division will not be satisfactory.

   Take the case of Messrs Harris and Gardner who put £9,000 and £1,000, respectively, into their partnership. In the first year they make a profit of £2,000. If they shared the profits equally, both would receive £1,000; but if the share was in the same ratio as their capital, Harris would get £1,800 and Gardner £200. Clearly an equal division would be in Gardner's interest. But suppose it had been a loss of £10,000 instead? Now an equal division would weigh heavily against Gardner. His initial investment of £1,000 would have incurred a cost of £5,000, leaving him £4,000 down over all; while Harris would still have £4,000 left. Anyone joining a business as a minor partner would be well advised to check the profit/loss division carefully.

3   It is quite normal for partners to receive interest on the capital they have invested in the business — particularly where different amounts of capital are involved. The interest — generally geared to bank rates — is paid before the profits are split — and the division of these should reflect the fact that the partners have already received a return on their investments.

Let's look at Harris and Gardner again. Suppose they agree upon an interest rate of 10%, and equal shares of the residue. What happens if they make a nett profit of £12,000?

	Harris	Gardner	Total
Capital	9,000	1,000	10,000
Interest	900	100	1,000
Profit Share	5,500	5,500	11,000
Total Received	6,400	5,600	12,000

Under this arrangement, the interest received is the reward for the capital investment, while the profit share is the reward for the hard work that both have put into the business.

4   The profit share will only happen at the end of the accounting period, but partners may want, or need, cash before then. How is that to be managed? Drawings — as an advance on profit — salary, or both?

Interest can be charged upon partners' drawings — those monies or goods withdrawn from the business for personal use. It is the flip side of paying interest on capital. Many partnerships do not bother about this, but others do because it discourages drawings. The less that is withdrawn from a business, the more remains for future growth.

Harris and Gardner, who are getting very organised in their partnership arrangements, have agreed that drawings should incur an interest charge, at the favourable rate of 0.5% per month (or 6% per annum) By the end of the year, their accounts show these positions:

End of Period Accounts

Harris

Drawings		Interest	
	£		£
1 Jan	100	100 * 0.5% * 12 =	6
1 Apr	200	200 * 0.5% * 9 =	9
1 Jul	400	400 * 0.5% * 6 =	12
1 Nov	300	300 * 0.5% * 2 =	3
TOTAL	1,000	TOTAL =	30

Gardner

Drawings		Interest	
	£		£
1 Jan	100	100 * 0.5% * 12 =	6
1 Mar	100	100 * 0.5% * 10 =	5
1 May	100	100 * 0.5% * 8 =	4
1 Sept	200	200 * 0.5% * 4 =	4
1 Dec	200	200 * 0.5% * 1 =	1
TOTAL	700	TOTAL =	20

Both the drawings and the interest charges must be taken into account in the end of the year settlement. The charges will be added to the Nett Profit of the firm, and the drawings will also be added back into it before the profit is shared.

There is one more aspect of partnerships that we could look at before returning to our example, and that is partners' salaries.

5   Where the partners contribute different amounts of time to the firm, a salary arrangement may be the fairest form of reward. If one partner works full time in the business, and the other only part time, it is only reasonable that the first should receive a full time salary. However, it must be noted that the salaries cannot be treated as an expense in the same way that employees' wages can. In accounting terms a salary is an agreed interest-free drawing against the possible profits of the firm.

Just how the salary is calculated is a matter for the partnership to decide. It could be a set monthly sum, or be based on an hourly rate, or on commission on sales. In our example partnership, Gardner works fulltime for the firm and takes a salary of £4,000. Harris puts in far less time, and takes only half a share of the profits.

We can now draw up a full Trading, Profit and Loss Appropriation Account for the Harris-Gardner partnership. (Note that, by convention, the word 'Appropriation' is not normally included in the title.) The first part – up to the calculation of Nett Profit – is the same as for a sole trader. We shall pick it up from that point.

		£	£	£
Nett Profit				12,000
Add Interest Charged on Drawings				
	Harris		30	
	Gardner		20	50
				12,050
Less Salary:	Gardner		4,000	
Less Interest on Capital				
	Harris	900		
	Gardner	100	1,000	5,000
				7,050
Balance of Profits Shared				
	Harris 50%		3,525	
	Gardner 50%		3,525	7,050

The £12,000 Nett Profits have been shared:

	Harris	Gardner
Balance of Profits	3,525	3,525
Interest on Capital	900	100
Salary		4,000
	4,425	7,625
Less Interest on Drawings	30	20
	4,395	7,605
Harris	4,395	
Gardner	7,605	
	12,050	

Capital and Current Accounts

The partnership must decide how salaries, profit and interest are to be treated within the accounts, and there are essentially two alternatives here. The Capital Accounts can be *Fixed* or *Fluctuating*.

End of Period Accounts

1. In a *Fixed Capital* – as the name suggests – the capital sum remains for the most part constant. The only variation will come when a partner chooses to raise or reduce his or her investment in the business. With this arrangement, a Current Account is needed to record profits, interest and salaries. Hence, if Harris and Gardner used this system, their books would show these positions by the end of the year.

HARRIS CAPITAL ACCOUNT

Date	Details	£
Jan 1	Bank	9,000

GARDNER CAPITAL ACCOUNT

Date	Details	£
Jan 1	Bank	1,000

HARRIS CURRENT ACCOUNT

Date	Details	£	Date	Details	£
Dec 31	Yearly Drawings	1,000	Dec 31	P & L Appropriation	
Dec 31	P & L Appropriation			Interest on Capital	900
	Interest on Drawings	30		Share of Profits	3,525
	Balance	3,395			
		4,425			4,425

GARDNER CURRENT ACCOUNT

Date	Details	£	Date	Details	£
Dec 31	Yearly Drawings	700	Dec 31	P & L Appropriation	
Dec 31	P & L Appropriation			Interest on Capital	100
	Interest on Drawings	20		Share of Profits	3,525
	Balance	6,905		Salary	4,000
		7,625			7,625

You will see that the monies that the partners have already taken from the business or which they owe to it (Drawings and Interest Charged) have been debited, and that which is due to them (Interest on Capital, Profit Share and Salary) is credited. You might also notice that

End of Period Accounts

although Share of Profits is written into these accounts here, it cannot, of course, be determined until the Trading, Profit and Loss Accounts have been drawn up.

2 *Fluctuating Capital Accounts* are an alternative to Fixed Capital and Current accounts, though this latter arrangement is generally preferred. With a fluctuating Capital Account, the interest, profit and salary transactions are all recorded there. Perhaps one advantage of this system is that if the money a partner takes out of the business exceeds the capital sum, then the account will show a Debit balance. In a Sage accountancy system, this could be easily spotted in the Trial Balance display.

The transfer to computer

There is a fixed layout to the final accounts in the Sage accountancy systems, with the Nett Profit always appearing as the final item on the Profit and Loss Account. The Balance Sheet is then produced directly afterwards, with no opportunity to insert an Appropriation Account. It is therefore not possible to use the same presentation – or sequence of calculations – used in a manual system. There is also the added complication that, by law, any monies that the partners take from the firm – the key concern of the appropriation accounts – must not be deducted within the Profit and Loss Account.

Perhaps the simplest solution is to bypass the Profit and Loss Appropriation Account altogether and include the partners' deductions from the firm (both drawings and salary) only in the Balance Sheet. The other considerations – interest calculations and the profit split – can then be added afterwards, by hand. The calculations needed for these will have to be done outside of the system anyway, as the accountancy packages have no facilities for this kind of computation.

This is quite acceptable from an accounting point of view. The details of the partners' transactions with the firm must be shown somewhere within the final accounts; but they don't have to appear twice – which is what happens in most manual systems.

An alternative approach is to run the Profit and Loss and Balance Sheet routine twice; first to produce an accurate Profit and Loss Account, and then – after appropriations have been made – to get a Balance Sheet on which the partners' relationships with the firm are detailed. To do this you will need to set up an Appropriation Account within the Nominal

End of Period Accounts

Ledger. When the Nett Profit has been found, from the first run, this will be transferred to the Appropriation Account as a Credit entry. (The balancing Debit entry will be in the Bank.)

The other accounts that will be needed in any given firm will depend upon the complexity of the partnership's financial arrangements and the degree of information needed in the reports from the system. It is important to remember that while the records of individual transactions are kept within specific accounts, only the balances show up in the Trial Balance and the Management Reports. So, each item that you want to have visible in those outputs must have its own account.

A single Fluctuating Capital account for each partner is unlikely to be enough, for you need to be able to make the distinction between those transactions that have taken place during the accounting year and past capital investment.

The addition of a Current account will make this split possible, but for the fullest reporting you will need separate Interest, Drawings, Profit Share and Salary accounts for each partner. The nature of the entries will be the same whether in a Current account or a set of separate ones. Here we have used just the Current.

Drawings	Debit Current	Credit Bank
Salary	Credit Current	Debit Appropriation
Interest on Capital	Credit Current	Debit Appropriation
Interest Charged	Debit Current	Credit Appropriation
Profit Share	Credit Current	Debit Appropriation

After these Journal Entries have been completed, the Appropriations account should be in balance.

APPROPRIATION ACCOUNT

Salary (Gardner)	4,000	Nett Profit (Bank)	12,000
Interest on Capital (H)	900	Interest Charged (Harris)	30
Interest on Capital (G)	100	Interest Charged (Gardner)	20
Profit Share (Harris)	3,525		
Profit Share (Gardner)	3,525		
	12,050		12,050

If the Current account method is used, then the partners will have readily available summaries of their financial transactions with the firm, but only the balance will appear on the Balance Sheet. The individual account approach does provide a higher level of information.

When the Accounts Print-out routine is run again, the Appropriation Account will have no effect as it is in balance, but the Nett Profit will have been reduced to zero as it has been allocated to the partners. This does not matter as we are not interested in the Profit and Loss Account on this second run. The focus this time will be on the Balance Sheet, and the partners' accounts will appear there in place of the single Nett Profit figure, as you will see in the next section.

Appropriation Accounts and the Limited Company

The Appropriation Account of a company is completely different from that of a partnership because of the way that profits are split. In a partnership, all the profits are shared out. If the partners wish, they can plough back some of their returns in the form of additional capital – but that is another matter. In a company, the business will normally pay out some of the profit as dividends to its shareholders, and retain some for the future.

We will base our first set of examples on a company called Dee Distribution. It has an ordinary share capital of £100,000, and a 5% preference share capital of £10,000. In its first year of trading made a nett profit of £20,000. The business was able to meet its obligation to the preference shareholders, and the directors decided to pay a dividend of 10% to the ordinary shareholders. Thus we see:

Profit & Loss Appropriation Account for the year ending 31 Dec. 198-

	£	£
Nett Profit		20,000
Less Proposed Dividends:		
Preference Dividend 5%	500	
Ordinary Dividend 10%	10,000	10,500
Balance of Unappropriated Profit		9,500

The Unappropriated Profit would be carried forward to the next year, where it would be added to the Nett Profit – or, more significantly, might offset any Nett Loss.

The company may also decide to create *Reserve accounts,* in which profits are held for future capital expenditure or cash needs. *Fixed Asset*

End of Period Accounts

Replacement Reserves are common features of company accounts. The money needed for new vehicles, plant and machinery, premises or furniture would come from here. A *'General Reserve'* will not have any specific purpose, but is there for a rainy day.

We can see these in use if we look at Dee Distribution's appropriation account for their second year. Profits were good enough to increase the ordinary dividend to 12%, and to allow the creation of reserve accounts.

Profit & Loss Appropriation Account for the year ending 31 Dec. 198-

	£	£
Balance of Unappropriated Reserve		9,500
Add Nett Profit		28,000
		37,500
Less Proposed Dividends:		
Preference Dividend 5%	500	
Ordinary Dividend 12%	12,000	
Less Transfer to Reserves		
Fixed Asset Replacement	10,000	
General Reserve	8,000	30,500
Balance of Unappropriated Profit		7,500

Over at Grunks Ltd, the picture is not so rosy, which will at least give us the opportunity to see how to handle a Nett Loss! Their capital, as you may recall, is composed of £200,000 ordinary share and £10,000 preference shares (at 7%). In their first year of trading, they made a Nett Loss of £46,300.

Profit and Loss Appropriation Account for the year ending 31 Dec. 198-

	£	£
(1) Nett Loss		(46,300)
Less Proposed Dividends:		
(2) Preference Dividend 5%	—	
Ordinary Dividend 10%	—	-
Balance of Unappropriated Loss		(46,300)

1 By convention, all losses are shown in brackets.
2 No profit, therefore no dividend, even for the preference shareholders.

End of Period Accounts

In the following year, the Gross Profit of almost £90,000 was reduced to £28,250 Nett — a small profit, but a significant turnaround on the first year's results. However, as you can see in the Appropriation Account, this was still not enough to outweigh the loss that had been carried forward.

Profit & Loss Appropriation Account for the year ending 31 Dec. 198-

	£	£
Balance of Unappropriated Loss		(46,300)
Nett Profit		28,250
		(18,050)
Less Proposed Dividends:		
Preference Dividend 5%	—	
Ordinary Dividend 10%	—	-
Balance of Unappropriated Loss		(18,050)

The transfer to computer

In practice, company appropriation accounts pose fewer problems than those of partnerships. There are no complications of Drawings or Interest, and directors' fees are a straightforward expense on the business.

The company will need Nominal Accounts for any reserves and the unappropriated profit/loss (located in the 'Financed By' section), and for the dividends paid on each type of share (located in Current Liabilities). The most awkward aspect is that of style, for — as we noted with partnerships — the Nett Profit is the last figure on the Profit and Loss Account, and the Reserves, Unappropriated Profit and Dividends cannot be allocated until this has been completed.

As with a partnership, the solution may be to run the Acounts Print-out routine once to get the Profit and Loss Account, then use Journal Entries to transfer money between the Appropriation and other accounts before running the Print-out a second time to get the Balance Sheet.

If it is important to the company that the presentation should follow the standard layout, then it is little trouble to copy figures across from the Sage print-out onto a new sheet. But in terms of accuracy and content, the style is irrelevant.

End of Period Accounts

The Balance Sheet

In a manual system, the Balance Sheet is completed after the Trading, Profit and Loss Appropriation Account, and provides a summary of the assets and liabilities of the business. As the name implies, this, like the Trial Balance, is where two sets of numbers agree – and, as before, the balance proves only that everything has been entered as a debit and credit. The fact that you can produce an accurate Balance Sheet does not prove that all transactions have been recorded correctly.

We will take the Balance Sheet in two parts. The first part deals with assets and liabilities, and its format is common to all types of businesses, though not all may have the full range of entries. The figures in this first example have been kept deliberately simple, as the focus here is on what goes into the sheet. Too much reality can be confusing.

Balance Sheet as at ....

		£	£	£
(1) Fixed Assets				
Premises				100,000
(2) Plant and Machinery	– Depreciation 40,000 – 5,000 =			35,000
Motor Vehicles	– Depreciation 12,000 – 2,000 =			10,000
Office Equipment	– Depreciation 5,500 – 500 =			5,000
				150,000
Add Current Assets (3)				
(4) Stock of Raw Materials			20,000	
Stock of Work in Progress			10,000	
Stock of Finished Goods			20,000	
Debtors			35,000	
(5) Pre-payments			5,000	
Bank			25,000	
Cash			5,000	
			120,000	
Less Current Liabilities (6)				
Creditors		18,000		
(7) Accruals		2,000		
(8) Corporation Tax		10,000		
(9) Dividend Proposed		15,000	45,000	
(10)	Working Capital		75,000	75,000
(11)				225,000

End of Period Accounts

1 Fixed Assets are items which have been bought to be retained within the business (for at least a year), and not for resale at a profit. They will normally be items which are needed in the running of the business.

2 There are two generally accepted methods of handling depreciation in the Balance Sheet of a manual system. The older way is to give the start of year value, the year's depreciation and the current value. This latter will then reappear as the start of year figure in the next Sheet.

More recently, the trend has been to show the original cost price and the total depreciation to date — accumulated over the years, and thence the resulting current value.

Whichever method is used, the net figures can never be entirely accurate as it is impossible to give an exact future resale value. When transferring to a computerised system, the simplest approach is to credit the depreciation against the value of the assets within their individual accounts, then bring these balances — the current values — directly into the Balance Sheet. The original values and the depreciation figures can then be drawn from the account histories and attatched as Notes to the Sheet if needed.

3 Current Assets are those that will be realised (turned to cash) within the course of the next year's trading. Note that they are listed in order of 'liquidity' — the ease with which they can be realised, and that the least liquid are at the top. The importance of this will become clear later when we look at ratios.

   (a) Stock   (Unsold goods)
   (b) Debtors   (Money owed to the business)
   (c) Prepayments (Money paid in advance)
   (d) Bank   (Money in the bank)
   (e) Cash   (Money in the till)

4 Only manufacturers will include all three types of stock. They are shown separately as they will be used as the Opening Stock values in the next year's books.

End of Period Accounts

5 Prepayments relate to goods paid for in advance. They will not show up in the Trial Balance, but first appear in Notes attached to it. As was stated earlier, all Notes must be entered twice. With Prepayments, the first entry is deducted from an expense in the Profit and Loss Account:

    e.g. Electricity   £200
         Less Prepaid   £60   £140

In the trial balance this was on the right, as a Credit; here it is on the left as an asset.

6 Current Liabilities are the reverse of Current Assets, in that they are items that will be paid off during the next year.

7 Accruals are the reverse of Prepayments, and in the same way appear first as a Note after the Trial Balance. There an accrual is a Debit entry, adding to an expense; here it is a liability.

8 Corporation Tax is only relevant in company accounts. With the sole trader or partnership, it is not the business which is taxed, but the individuals who own it.

9 The dividend to be distributed to shareholders is a Current Liability at this stage, as it has yet to be paid. Obviously this is a feature only of company accounts.

10 Working Capital is the difference between Current Assets and Current Liabilities. It is usually a plus figure. A minus value — unless there are particular circumstances — would be a cause for concern.

Note that if this were the Balance Sheet of a sole trader or partnership, the Working Capital would have been £100,000, as there would be no deductions for Corporation Tax or Dividends.

11 The final figure represents the Nett Asset value of the business.

End of Period Accounts

So far we have only been looking at the first half of the Balance Sheet. There should be no problems here when transferring to a Sage accountancy system. All that is necessary is to ensure that all the relevant accounts are included under the right headings when specifying the layout of the Balance Sheet.

The second half will provide the same final figure as the first, but this time it will show the ways in which the assets have been financed. Types of finance include Capital, Profits, Loans and Reserves (in limited companies). The format of this part of the sheet will depend upon the nature of the business – Sole Trader, Partnership or Limited Company.

Sole Trader Balance Sheet

		£	£	£
	Financed By:			
	Capital			100,000
	Add Nett Profit			75,000
				175,000
	Less Drawings			25,000
(1)				150,000
	Long-Term Liabilities:			
(2)	Bank Loan		40,000	
	Building Society Loan		60,000	100,000
				250,000

1. This sub-total shows the money that the owner has invested in the business, or left there as untouched profits during the year.
2. A bank loan or debenture that is to run for at least a year is counted as a long-term liability and a source of finance. In accounting terms it is quite different from a short-term loan or overdraft, both of which count as Current Liabilities and will appear in the first half of the Balance Sheet.

End of Period Accounts

The transfer to computer

The main point to note here is that in a Sage accounts package there is only the single heading 'Financed By' in this part of the sheet. Long-term Liabilities are therefore treated as another form of finance. As with the other parts of the Monthly Accounts, you can have up to fifteen categories under this heading, and each of these can cover a range of neighbouring accounts. Capital, Bank and other Loans should be included here, as should Drawings. This will be a Debit balance and will reduce the total. The system will automatically bring in the final figure from the Profit and Loss Account.

Financed by	Capital	100,000.00
	Bank Loan	40,000.00
	Building Society Loan	60,000.00
	Drawings	(25,000.00)
	Profit / Loss Account	75,000.00
		250,000.00

Partnership Balance Sheet

		£	£	£
Financed By:				
Capitals	Smith		75,000	
	Jones		25,000	100,000
Current Accounts		Smith	Jones	
Interest on Capital		7,500	2,500	
Share of Profits		33,000	33,000	
		40,500	35,500	
Less Drawings		10,000	15,000	
Interest on Drawings		400	600	
		30,100	19,900	50,000
				150,000
Long-Term Liabilities:				
Debenture			40,000	
Building Society Loan			60,000	100,000
				250,000

End of Period Accounts

The Capital and Current Accounts of each partner are included in the Balance Sheet, and from these it is possible to see who contributes what to the business. In this example, Smith not only provides more of the Capital, he also leaves more of his profit entitlement within the business during the year.

You might notice that the figures here are essentially the same as in the sole trader example, though the profit to be appropriated has become £66,000 (£75,000 Nett − £10,000 Interest on Capital + £1,000 Interest Charged).

The transfer to computer

We noted earlier, in the section on the Appropriation Accounts that there were essentially two approaches to handling partnership finances. In the minimal approach only those monies actually taken out of the business — the Drawings — are included in the Accounts Print-out, with the rest being handled outside of the computerised system. The second approach used an Appropriation Account, and necessitated a double run of the Print-out routines.

Let's start with the easy method! It is virtually the same as for a sole trader, with the only difference being that you will need to include the drawings accounts of each of the partners. Thus:

Financed by

Capital	100,000.00
Debenture	40,000.00
Building Society Loan	60,000.00
Drawings (Smith)	(10,000.00)
Drawings (Jones)	(15,000.00)
Profit / Loss Account	75,000.00
	250,000.00

Now let's take these same figures, but put them into a system where an Appropriation Account is completed after the Profit and Loss Account, and where there are separate Drawings, Interest on Capital, Interest Charged and Profit Share accounts for each partner. All of these partners' accounts will be included under the 'Financed By' heading so that a fuller picture emerges.

End of Period Accounts

Financed by

Capital	100,000.00
Debenture	40,000.00
Building Society Loan	60,000.00
Interest on Capital (Smith)	7,500.00
Interest on Capital (Jones)	2,500.00
Profit Share (Smith)	33,000.00
Profit Share (Smith)	33,000.00
Drawings (Smith)	(10,000.00)
Drawings (Jones)	(15,000.00)
Interest Charged (Smith)	(400.00)
Interest Charged (Jones)	(600.00)
Profit / Loss Account	0,000.00
	250,000.00

The Limited Company Balance Sheet

		£	£	£
	Financed By:			
(1)	Authorised Share Capital			150,000
(2)	Issued 90,000 Ordinary Shares of £1 each fully paid			90,000
	Issued 5,000 Preference Shares of £2 each fully paid			10,000
				100,000
	Reserves:			
	Fixed Asset Replacement		10,000	
	General Reserve		5,000	
(3)	Profit and Loss		10,000	25,000
	Long-Term Liabilities			
	Debentures		40,000	
	Bank Loan		60,000	100,000
				225,000

End of Period Accounts

1. Authorised Share Capital must be shown, by law, but it is not included in the calculations of the Balance Sheet. In practice many businesses will have issued fewer than their authorised number of shares. The authorised share capital may be altered during the life of the firm.

2. Here we see the details of the shares that have been issued — their number, face value and whether or not they have been fully paid. Shares are usually bought in stages, with a partial payment when the buyer first applies for shares and subsequent instalments after a period of a few months.

    The sum set aside for the dividends to be paid to shareholders will have been included in the first half of the Balance Sheet under Current Liabilities.

3. This is the undistributed profit or loss which will be carried forward into the next year's accounts.

The transfer to computer

The most obvious problem here is that it is not going to be possible to include the Authorised Share Capital in the Balance Sheet print-out, as any figures which are included will be worked into the calculations. For that matter, there is really not much point in holding a record of the Authorised Share Capital within the computerised system. This only deals with active accounts.

For the rest, the appropriation of profits can be managed in much the same way as in the partnership. The Nett Profit should be credited to the Appropriation Account, and from there to Tax, Dividend and Reserve accounts. The first two are brought into the sheet layout under the Current Liabilities heading, and the reserves under 'Financed By'. When the Accounts print-out is run for the second time, the Balance Sheet will then show all the necessary information.

4

Stock Control

Not all businesses have need of a stock control system. Those in the building trades, and some service industries will often have no 'stock' as such, but will buy materials as they are needed for particular jobs. But any retailer, wholesaler and manufacturer will be well aware of the importance of a good stock control system.

It is not just a matter of knowing what goods are in stock, where they are located and what needs reordering. Stock must be valued regularly for the accounts; and if the optimum times and quantities for reordering can be established, then there can be significant improvements in cash flow and profitability.

The amount of detail that is required in a stock control system will depend very largely on the value of the individual items. The furniture retailer will need to know exactly how many beds, tables, chairs and three-piece suites are in stock; he will therefore have to register each sale in the stock records as it happens, or very shortly afterwards. But it would be ridiculous for the family grocer to record each tin of beans that was sold. The time and effort involved would simply not justify it. Here it is sufficient to know that there are enough unopened cases in the store room to keep the shelves stocked until the next delivery. (Though the till-updated stock systems that are now used in the bigger stores and supermarkets could soon be cheap enough for even the smaller shopkeepers.)

Stock Control

Stock Valuations

If goods could always be bought at the same price, then stock valuations would be much simpler. Unfortunately, that is not the case. In times of high inflation, stock prices may rise several times a year; and when competition is rife in a sector of the market, special offers and discounts may produce a different price with each order. Even when prices are stable, the actual delivered cost may vary from time to time depending upon the size of an order, carriage and other incidental costs.

Any stock control system must therefore be able to cope with a multiplicity of cost prices for each line of goods in stock. There are three approaches to the question of which prices to use, both for setting sale prices and for stock valuations. They are normally referred to as *FIFO*, *LIFO* and *AVCO*.

FIFO stands for *First In First Out*. This is based on the assumption that when you are fulfilling an order, you will take from the shelves those items that have been there longest. In practice, this is what generally happens, especially where the goods are perishable. Any retailer who did not use the earliest 'Sell-by' dates first would soon run into the problem of out-of-date stock.

FIFO users have to watch their margins. If the mark-up on the cost price is relatively low, and prices are rising rapidly, then the sale price of goods may be uncomfortably close to the latest cost prices.

LIFO stands for *Last In First Out*. The approach is not much favoured in Britain, though it is more widely used in the United States. As the goods that are sold are costed at the latest – and presumably highest – price, LIFO tends to understate the Gross Profit on sales; and with more of the unsold stock being at the earlier – and lower – prices, it will give a lower stock valuation. At times of high inflation, such a cautious approach has something to commend it.

AVCO is *AVerage COst*. This works by taking the total value of all the items in stock – at their original cost price – and dividing it by the number to get an average cost for each item. It thus cuts a central path between FIFO and LIFO in the values it produces for the accounts. It also has the distinct advantage of simplicity of operation, as it avoids the complicated costings that occur with either of the other systems when an order has to be fulfilled with stock from different deliveries. The Stock Control modules in Popular Accounts Plus (PCW), Accountant Plus (PC) and Financial Controller (PC) use the AVCO method.

Stock Control

How do these different systems affect the stock valuation and the gross profits? Let's take the case of a toy retailer and focus on his stock of roller skates. They are completely out of stock after Christmas, so he buys ten pairs in January, at £10 each. Five pairs are sold during that month, and he reorders another ten at the start of February. This time the price has risen to £12. He sells four more that month. For various reasons, including local competition and a long-running advertising campaign, the sale price stays at £15 throughout this time.

```
PURCHASES                          SALES
January    10 * £10 = £100         5 * £15 =    £75
February   10 * £12 = £120         4 * £15 =    £60
                      ----                      ----
                      £220                      £135
```

FIFO
    Cost of Sales   9 * £10 =   £90
    Gross Profit   £135 − 90 =   £45
    Stock value 28th Feb   1 * £10 + 10 * £12 =   £130

LIFO
    Cost of Sales   9 * £12 =   £108
    Gross Profit   £135 − 108 =   £27
    Stock value 28th Feb   10 * £10 + 1 * £12 =   £112

AVCO
    Average cost   (10 * £10 + 10 * £12) / 20 =   £11
    Cost of Sales   9 * £11 =   £99
    Gross Profit   £135 − 99 =   £36
    Stock value   28th Feb 11 * £11 =   £121

Finding the Average Cost
Average cost is computed on an on-going basis. As each new delivery is made, the cost and number of items are added to those of the existing stock, and the new average is calculated. So, if our toy retailer took delivery of another ten pairs of roller skates in March — with the price now £13.20, the calculations would be:

	Current	New Delivery	Updated
Stock Value	£121	£132	£252
Stock numbers	11	10	21
Average Cost	£11	£13.20	£12

Some months afterwards, when he is down to his last five pairs, he has a new delivery — ten pairs still at £13.20.

Stock Control

	Current	New Delivery	Updated
Stock Value	£60	£132	£192
Stock numbers	5	10	15
Average Cost	£12	£13.20	£12.80

You should notice two things from this sequence. First, that you do not have to keep going back to the earliest cost price – the calculations use the current average and the new price only; second, that the AVCO approach has a smoothing effect on price rises.

Of course, if you are using a Sage software package, you will not have to perform these calculations – the system will do them for you, but it is perhaps useful to know what is going on. If all sales and purchases are recorded via the Invoicing routines then Financial Controller will automatically keep stock levels up to date – and it will tell you whether or not an order can be met from stock as you are making out a Sales Invoice. It will also tell you what items have reached, or fallen below, the Reorder level – but it will not work out for you what that reorder level should be, nor how much stock to order at a time. These are calculations that must be made outside of the system.

Economic Stock Levels

The *Economic Order Quantity* (or EOQ) represents a balance between the cost of keeping items in stock and the cost of reordering. It is the number of items that should be ordered at any one time – providing that cost is the only consideration. This is an important proviso, for there are other variables such as the availability of storage space, the reliability of supply and the irregularity of use, amongst others. All of these will affect the order size. Here we are focusing on the single aspect of cost.

The EOQ can be found either by a formula or by graphing. There are advantages in both methods. The formula is quick and easy to apply, but the graph approach gives a better picture of the situation. This can be seen by working through both methods using the same data.

In the example firm, a total of 2,000 of a certain item of stock is used each year. The unit price of the item is £12.00, and it has been established that the carrying cost of the line is £4.00 per item. (i.e. the cost of the storage space, handling charges, insurance, breakages and similar in-store costs average out at £4.00 per item per year). It is also known that the total costs incurred by each reorder and delivery are £80.00.

Stock Control

The EOQ formula is:

$$\sqrt{\left(2 * \text{Ordering Cost} * \frac{\text{Annual Usage}}{\text{Carrying Cost}}\right)}$$

This gives the answer SQRT(2 * 80 * 2,000/4) = SQRT(80,000) = 282.3. You do not, of course, want fractions of items, and in practice the EOQ would be rounded to the closest quantity that the distributors are willing to supply. Here it would probably be taken as 300.

What this formula does not show is how far you can deviate from this figure without the cost changing significantly. Would it make much difference if stock was ordered in quantities of 200 or 500? The formula does not tell you. There are other things that the formula does not reveal, such as the average level of stock at that EOQ, and the total costs involved.

The graphing method provides a higher degree of information, but takes a little more time to set up. To produce the graph, such as the one shown here, you need to generate a table of figures. A spreadsheet would be useful for this, though it does not take long to work it out by hand.

The basis of the calculation is:

ORDER QUANTITY	A suitable range of possible values
NO. OF ORDERS	Annual Usage/Order Quantity
ANNUAL ORDER COST	No. of Orders * Cost of ordering and delivery
AVERAGE STOCK	here it is taken to be half the Order Quantity. It assumes that the items will be out of stock by the time the delivery arrives, and that usage rates are constant.
CARRYING COST	Average stock * Unit carrying cost
TOTAL COST	Annual Order Cost + Carrying Cost

ORDER QUANTITY	100	200	300	400	500
NO. OF ORDERS	20	10	7	5	4
ANNUAL ORDER COST	£1600	£800	£560	£400	£320
AVERAGE STOCK	50	100	150	200	250
CARRYING COST	£200	£400	£600	£800	£1000
TOTAL COST	£1800	£1200	£1100	£1200	£1320

Stock Control

With smaller steps between the order quantities – 100, 150, 200, 250, 300... more accurate results can be obtained, but even with this simple table a pattern can be seen. If the figures from the Cost lines are plotted on a graph, then the relationships will be made clearer.

It will be seen that as the size of the orders rise, the overall Ordering Cost declines, but the Carrying Costs rise in line with them. The Total cost figures form a curve, and it is at the lowest point of this curve that you will find the EOQ. Here the lowest figure is aroung 300 units, but what is also clear is that the total cost does not vary that much anywhere between 200 and 400.

Reorder and Safety Stock Level

These stock levels – that at which a new order should be originated and that below which the stock should not be allowed to fall – can be established in several ways. Some methods are more complex, though more systematic, than others. All require that the firm has been able to collect figures of rates of usage and delivery over a period.

Daily Usage	No. of Days
5	3
6	5
7	10
8	14
9	11
10	4
11	2
12	1
Total	50
Mean Usage	8 per day

Lead Time	Frequency
10	2
11	4
12	6
13	4
14	3
15	2
Total	20
Mean Lead Time	12 days

Stock Control

At the simplest, the reorder level can be calculated by multiplying the maximum daily usage by the maximum lead time on delivery. On that basis, even if the delivery took the maximum number of days to get through, and the stock was used at its maximum rate throughout the lead time, it would only run out as the new stock arrived.

You then find the *Average Usage* during lead time, by multiplying the Mean Daily Use by the Mean Lead Time. The Safety, or Minimum, stock level is then the reorder level less the Average Usage. If stock gets this low, it is time for action!

So, using the figures given here:

    Reorder Level = 12 * 15 = 180
    Average Usage = 8 * 12 = 96
    Safety Level = 180 – 96 = 84

This is a rough and ready system, and should be sufficient for those firms in which there is little to be gained by fine-tuning the inventory management. Where there is a high turnover of stock, and a great deal of capital tied up in it, then the more precision that can be applied in this area, the better.

As was mentioned earlier, the Stock Control software will not make these calculations for you. However, the system does record delivery dates, and usage on a month-to-date and year-to-date basis. It should therefore be simple enough to collect the data that is needed to work out the Reorder Levels and Economic Order Quantities of your stock lines.

Stock Control and The Computer

The User Manual explains the operations in this area very well, but there are perhaps a few points worth stressing.

Financial Controller's stock system allows you to hold a great deal of valuable information about each stock line – rather more than could be conveniently managed in a manual system. It is not simply a matter of recording numbers in stock, purchase and sales price and store locations. The software also holds details of reorder levels and quantities, up to three rates of discount, the Nominal code of the relevant Sales account, the appropriate VAT code and the supplier's reference.

Stock Control

As was noted earlier, it also stores the numbers and values of sales to date, and the dates of the last sale and purchase transactions. There is a further feature, which we will return to shortly, that allows you to link together the components that makeup a multi-part sales unit – the monitor, disk drives and keyboard that comprise a computer installation, or the items in a HiFi system.

The Stock Control module is designed to be used alongside the other modules; and in the normal course of events most of the information used by the Stock routines will be gleaned from the Sales and Purchase Invoicing and Order Processing routines.

However, it can be run in isolation – which may be useful when first transferring to a computerised system. Just using the software to manage the stock – and not any other part of the accounts – is quite a good way to gain familiarity with the computer. Where this is being done, stock levels can be updated after a sale or purchase by using the Adjustments In and Out options.

Where the sales items consist of sets of interchangeable sub-components, this can pose particular problems for stock management. Stacking HiFi systems illustrate this point well. Take the situation where a shop stocks two types of amplifiers, four sizes of loudspeakers, double and single tape decks, a variety of turntables and pick-up arms, two qualities of compact disk player and VHF and long/medium waveband tuners – all from the same manufacturer and compatible with each other. Given that a dozen or more alternative systems can be assembled from this selection, how many of what are there in stock?

With the Financial Controller Control system, components can be linked into sales units. The software will check that all the necessary items are available, allocate them to the finished unit and calculate the total cost price. This can be done in advance, or as a sale is being made. The Stock Explosion report will give a detailed list of all assembled items for reference.

5

The Interpretation of Accounts

Accounting is not just concerned with the recording of transactions. It is also concerned with the overall financial health and progress of a business. How is the firm using its financial resources? What kind of a return is it making on its capital? What is the level of profit on its sales? How are the figures changing month by month and year by year? These are among the questions that anyone who runs a business should be asking, and the answers can be found in the accounts.

The most important technique for interpreting accounts is *Ratio Analysis.* The ratios – the relationships between numbers – obtained by comparing certain key figures, can provide a great deal of valuable information about the business.

There are several types of ratios, each of which reveals a different aspect of the business's performance. The ones we are concerned with here are those that show Liquidity, Profitability, Return on Capital and Use of Assets.

Liquidity Ratios

These indicate the liquidity of the business – i.e. its ability to find cash to meet short-term debts. There are three in common use.

The Interpretation of Accounts

The *Current Ratio* is a comparison of Current Assets and Current Liabilities. This figure is found – as are all ratios – by division. So, if the Assets stand at £140,000 and the Liabilities at £100,000 the ratio is:

$$\frac{\text{Current Assets}}{\text{Current Liabilities}} = \frac{140,000}{100,000} = 1.4 \text{ to } 1$$

If this business could realise all its current assets, it could pay off its current liabilities 1.4 times. In practice, this is probably not as healthy as it may sound. The ideal current ratio is generally taken to be between 1.5:1 and 2:1, but it must be remembered that stock is included among the assets. How the stock is valued, and the speed with which it can be turned into cash or trade debtors will affect the overall liquidity of the business.

The Quick Assets Ratio

This is also called the *Acid Test Ratio* as it seeks to answer the crucial question of what happens if the creditors all demand payment immediately. Stock is left out of the equation, on the assumption that it could not be sold fast enough to make any difference. It is also normal to leave out those liabilities that will not fall due within three months. Following on from the previous example, if the assets include stock of £50,000 and long-term liabilities of £5,000, then the quick assets ratio would be:

$$\frac{\text{Cash + Debtors + Cashable Investments}}{\text{Short-term Current Liabilities}} = \frac{£90,000}{£95,000} = 0.95 \text{ to } 1$$

Ideally it should be at least 1:1, and if it is not then the business should arrange overdraft facilities. While it is highly unlikely that all the creditors will want payment quickly, some of them certainly will. As it is equally unlikely that all debtors will pay quickly, there could be a cash flow problem.

Profitability Ratios

These focus on the profit made on sales. They are normally expressed as percentages rather than ratios.

The Interpretation of Accounts

Sales Margin
This is used where the operating costs – the administration, selling and distribution expenses – must be regarded as fixed, no matter what the sales volume. Given Sales of £50,000, Cost of Sales £40,000 and therefore Gross Profit of £10,000, the ratio would be:

$$\frac{\text{Gross Profit}}{\text{Sales}} = \frac{£10,000}{£50,000} = 20\%$$

The ratio should remain much the same over time, but will be affected by price-cutting, changes in the mix of goods that are sold where these have different margins, and by alterations in stock valuations and cut-off (that will affect the cost of sales).

There is no ideal ratio. The percentage can drop very low where stock turnover is high, and the business could still flourish.

Profit Volume
This is an alternative to the Sales Margin Ratio, and can be used where it is possible to separate out those costs that are directly related to the volume of sales. Commission, carriage and packing costs are typical variable expenses. These should be deducted from the Gross Profit to find the Contribution.

e.g.
	£
Sales	100,000
Cost of Sales	75,000
Variable Costs	10,000
Contribution	15,000

This produces the ratio:

$$\frac{\text{Contribution}}{\text{Sales}} = \frac{£15,000}{£100,000} = 15\%$$

This has the same limitations and the same range of viable results as the Sales Margin Ratio, but can give a ready guide to the performance of the business if worked out on a regular basis.

Nett Profit

The third of the profitability ratios works in exactly the same way as the others, though here Nett Profit is compared with Sales. This would normally show more variation if calculated month by month, as expenses are not always spread evenly through the year.

Return on Capital Employed

The ROCE ratio compares profits and assets. There are several varieties of this, of which the simplest is given by:

$$\frac{\text{Nett Profit}}{\text{Total Assets}}$$

This may be sufficient for a small trader, and will provide a rough and ready guide even where the accounts are more complex.

A more sophisticated version is:

$$\frac{\text{Operating Profit}}{\text{Operating Assets}}$$

Where Operating Profit is defined as Gross Profit less operating expenses, but before tax, investment income, interest on loans and any extraordinary items are taken into account. Operating Assets are fixed assets, stock and debtors. Cash and investments are ignored. The focus is, therefore, on the business's trading position.

The ratio is expressed as a percentage, so that where the profit was £10,000 and the assets £100,000 the ROCE would be 10%. This should be compared, on the one hand, with the return on alternative investments – where the business is entirely financed by the owners, would the capital earn more in a Building Society or shares? On the other hand, compared over time, the ROCE will give an indication of the growth of the business. It should be noted that where assets are stated at their historic or depreciated values, this will tend to improve the ROCE. Regular revaluation is essential if year by year comparisons are to be meaningful.

The Interpretation of Accounts

Use of Assets

These ratios indicate the efficiency with which the business is using its assets to generate sales, and thence cash.

Stock Turnover
This is calculated by:

$$\frac{\text{Cost of Goods Sold}}{\text{Average Stock}}$$

Where Average Stock is found by:

$$\frac{\text{Opening Stock} + \text{Closing Stock}}{2}$$

It shows the number of times a year that the business sells and completely replaces its stock. For example, a firm has an annual Cost of Goods Sold of £50,000, Opening Stock of £8,000 and Closing Stock of £12,000. Its *Turnover Ratio* is therefore:

$$\frac{50,000}{(8,000 + 12,000)/2} = \frac{50,000}{10,000} = 5 \text{ times a year}$$

The result will vary widely between businesses. The butcher, baker and greengrocer should have turnover on almost a daily basis, but a jeweller could operate profitably with a turnover as low as twice a year. As with so many of these ratios, the important comparisons are made over time. Is the firm improving, or at least maintaining, its turnover?

Credit Control
Credit Control works both ways. On the one hand the business needs to ensure that customers pay reasonably promptly, but without undue harassment; and on the other, it should take advantage of credit offered by suppliers but without putting those credit facilities in jeopardy by paying too slowly. There are two ratios which can help in this respect.

The average time that customers take to settle their bills can be found by:

$$\frac{\text{Trade Debtors}}{\text{Credit Sales}} * 365$$

The Interpretation of Accounts

With debtors of £8,000 and credit sales of £100,000, this would give 0.08 * 365 = 29.2 days. Given a credit period of 30 days, this ratio would fall within the normal, acceptable limits. If the ratio rose over 30 days, then it would be worth examining specific late debts. As the ratio approaches twice the credit period, the likelihood of debts proving to be irrecoverable grows alarmingly.

The same analysis can be performed with Trade Creditors and Credit Purchases. The two ratios should be much the same.

If we apply the ratios to a couple of our sample businesses, we should be able to make an assessment of their performances.

Palfreman Motor Spares

The key figures	Year 1	Year 2
Current Assets	49,100	53,500
Current Liabilities	6,000	5,250
Opening Stock	-	11,000
Closing Stock	11,000	30,000
Sales	116,000	112,000
Credit Sales	72,000	71,000
Cost of Goods Sold	73,000	69,250
Gross Profit	43,000	42,750
Nett Profit	20,300	19,900
Trade Debtors	15,000	17,500

Ratio Analysis

Current Ratio
Year 1
$$\frac{\text{Current Assets}}{\text{Current Liabilities}} = \frac{49,100}{6,000} = 8.2 \text{ to } 1$$

This is far higher than it needs to be, and should be investigated. Either too much money is sitting idly in the bank, or Palfreman is overstocked, or he is not chasing his debtors vigorously enough, or he is not taking full advantage of his suppliers' credit facilities. Most likely it is a combination of some or all of these.

The Interpretation of Accounts

Year 2

$$\frac{\text{Current Assets}}{\text{Current Liabilities}} = \frac{53{,}500}{5{,}250} = 10.2 \text{ to } 1$$

The ratio has worsened and must be tackled urgently.

The Quick Assets Ratio

Year 1

$$\frac{\text{Current Assets} - \text{Stock}}{\text{Current Liabilities}} = \frac{38{,}100}{6{,}000} = 6.4 \text{ to } 1$$

When stock is taken out of the reckoning, the ratio improves, but is still far above the ideal 1 to 1. The problem must therefore lie with cash holdings or credit control.

Year 2

$$\frac{\text{Current Assets} - \text{Stock}}{\text{Current Liabilities}} = \frac{23{-}500}{5{,}250} = 4.5 \text{ to } 1$$

This is substantially better than the Current Ratio for Year 2, and suggests that overstocking was a principal cause of that high value.

Sales Margin

Year 1

$$\frac{\text{Gross Profit}}{\text{Sales}} = \frac{43{,}000}{116{,}000} = 37.1\%$$

This is a realistic margin for relatively slow moving stock. The business clearly has a good potential for profitability.

Year 2

$$\frac{\text{Gross Profit}}{\text{Sales}} = \frac{42{,}750}{112{,}000} = 38.2\%$$

The figures are virtually the same as the previous year. While there has been no growth, at least Palfreman seems to have established a viable place in the market.

The Interpretation of Accounts

Return on Capital Employed
Year 1

$$\frac{\text{Nett Profit}}{\text{Total Assets}} = \frac{20{,}300}{49{,}100} = 41.3\%$$

This is an excellent first year result, showing a handsome return on capital. The slight drop in the next year is not particularly worrying as the ROCE ratio is still very high.

Year 2

$$\frac{\text{Nett Profit}}{\text{Total Assets}} = \frac{19{,}900}{53{,}500} = 37.2\%$$

Stock Turnover
Year 1

$$\frac{\text{Cost of Goods Sold}}{\text{Average Stock}} = \frac{73{,}000}{11{,}000} = 6.6 \text{ times}$$

This is a good figure. It means that even though Palfreman must carry a wide range of stock to meet any potential demand rapidly, the average spare part will sit on the shelves for less than two months before being sold.

Year 2

$$\frac{\text{Cost of Goods Sold}}{\text{Average Stock}} = \frac{69{,}250}{20{,}500} = 3.4 \text{ times}$$

As we suspected when comparing the Current and Quick Asset ratios, the stock holding has been much higher in this second year. This point is made more forcibly here with turnover dropping to almost half of its previous level.

The Interpretation of Accounts

Credit Control
Year 1

$$\frac{\text{Trade Debtors}}{\text{Credit Sales}} * 365 = \frac{15{,}000}{72{,}000} * 365 = 76 \text{ days}$$

Here then is a major source of Palfreman's over-high liquidity ratios. If his debtors are taking an average of 76 days to pay, then there is a very real danger that too many will turn into bad debts. Even if they do not, the simple fact is that money which is owing should be money which is earning.

Year 2

$$\frac{\text{Trade Debtors}}{\text{Credit Sales}} * 365 = \frac{13{,}500}{71{,}000} * 365 = 69 \text{ days}$$

This is not a real improvement – it could be due to a single customer paying up just before the end of the year, rather than after. It is still far too high.

The Interpretation?
While there is a good sound base for Palfreman's business, there are problem areas that are going to hinder its future success if not tackled rapidly. He could start by setting up a proper Stock Control system and establishing the rates of sale of different lines, and thence the economic reorder levels and quanitities. Reminder letters should be sent out to overdue customers on a regular basis – most people only need reminding of their debts. Both of these could be handled very competently by Accountant Plus or Financial Controller.

The Interpretation of Accounts

TWO-TONE CASH & CARRY

The key figures	Year 1	Year 2
Current Assets	128,500	174,500
Current Liabilities	47,300	78,000
Opening Stock	–	75,000
Closing Stock	75,000	95,000
Sales	504,000	622,000
Credit Sales	95,000	120,000
Trade Debtors	10,000	11,200
Cost of Goods Sold	402,000	481,000
Gross Profit	102,000	141,000
Nett Profit	42,500	80,650

Ratio Analysis

Current Ratio
Year 1

$$\frac{\text{Current Assets}}{\text{Current Liabilities}} = \frac{128{,}500}{47{,}300} = 2.7 \text{ to } 1$$

This is slightly on the high side, but not unreasonably so. It is inevitably difficult to get things absolutely right in the first year of a business. The market is still being tested, and relationships with customers and suppliers are not yet properly established. It is significant here that in the second year, the Current Ratio comes much closer to the ideal.

Year 2

$$\frac{\text{Current Assets}}{\text{Current Liabilities}} = \frac{174{,}500}{78{,}000} = 2.2 \text{ to } 1$$

The Quick Assets Ratio
Year 1

$$\frac{\text{Current Assets} - \text{Stock}}{\text{Current Liabilities}} = \frac{53{,}500}{47{,}300} = 1.1 \text{ to } 1$$

The Interpretation of Accounts

Once stock is removed, the ratio approaches the ideal. This suggests that the business is keeping reasonable control over credit, and that its cash holdings are not excessive. The same ratio is maintained in the second year.

Year 2

$$\frac{\text{Current Assets} - \text{Stock}}{\text{Current Liabilities}} = \frac{89,500}{78,000} = 1.1 \text{ to } 1$$

Sales Margin
Year 1

$$\frac{\text{Gross Profit}}{\text{Sales}} = \frac{102,000}{504,000} = 20.\%$$

While this is a lower margin than that enjoyed by Palfreman, the greater volume of sales should compensate for this. More important is the year on year comparison, and there we see that the margin has improved slightly in the subsequent period. As the firm becomes better established, they may not need to make so many special offers to attract new customers.

Year 2

$$\frac{\text{Gross Profit}}{\text{Sales}} = \frac{141,000}{622,000} = 22.6\%$$

Return on Capital Employed
Year 1

$$\frac{\text{Nett Profit}}{\text{Total Assets}} = \frac{42,500}{128,500} = 33.1\%$$

This good first year result puts the Sales Margin Ratio into context. It is the overall return on capital that counts, not the profit on sales. In the following year, this ratio improves to a very satisfactory 46%. The partnership is clearly prospering.

Year 2

$$\frac{\text{Nett Profit}}{\text{Total Assets}} = \frac{80{,}650}{174{,}500} = 46.2\%$$

Stock Turnover

Year 1

$$\frac{\text{Cost of Goods Sold}}{\text{Average Stock}} = \frac{402{,}000}{75{,}000} = 5.3 \text{ times}$$

This is not a bad result for the Cash and Carry. Its stocks of fresh, canned and packaged foods do move rather quicker than this would suggest, as the overall figure is brought down by slower moving items such as electrical equipment and toys. There is room for improvement, but in the context of the other ratios, there seems to be no cause for alarm. In the second year the ratio stays much the same – that minor variation could be caused by errors in stock valuation.

Year 2

$$\frac{\text{Cost of Goods Sold}}{\text{Average Stock}} = \frac{481{,}000}{85{,}000} = 5.6 \text{ times}$$

Credit Control

Year 1

$$\frac{\text{Trade Debtors}}{\text{Credit Sales}} * 365 = \frac{10{,}000}{95{,}000} * 365 = 38 \text{ days}$$

This is a little on the high side, but as credit sales represent only a fifth of all sales, it has only a limited effect on the business. While it is arguable that offering advantageous credit terms will bring in new custom, it may be more difficult later to bring credit under control without antagonising old customers. It is perhaps as well, therefore, to start as you mean to

The Interpretation of Accounts

continue. What we see here is that Two-Tone has managed to improve its credit control in the second year, and has increased the volume of its credit sales at the same time.

Year 2

$$\frac{\text{Trade Debtors}}{\text{Credit Sales}} * 365 = \frac{11,200}{120,000} * 365 = 34 \text{ days}$$

The Interpretation?
Two-Tone would appear to have got off to a very good start. Crucial ratios are being maintained at healthy levels, or being improved. The business is expanding quite rapidly and on a sound financial basis.

6

Sundry Considerations

Value Added Tax

VAT has turned the British from a nation of shopkeepers into a nation of tax collectors. Any business with a turnover in taxable goods or services above a certain threshold must register for VAT; and with the threshold currently at £20,500 that means that the vast majority of all businesses are working for H.M. Customs & Excise.

Of course, being VAT-registered does mean that you can claim back the tax paid on purchases and on some of the expenses of the business, but where taxable inputs are low, the savings may not really compensate for the extra work. And now for the good news – VAT is a breeze with the Financial Controller system. It does the donkey work of calculating Input and Output VAT and pulling together figures for the quarterly return. All you have to do is get the figures right when you record your transactions, and read off the values at the end of the quarter. If mistakes are made, they can be easily sorted out as long as you have a reasonable grasp of how VAT is handled within the accounts.

VAT is an indirect tax charged on the supply of goods and services. Currently there are only two rates of tax in the UK, though there are more

Sundry Considerations

than this in some other EEC countries – the tax is common to EEC members – and there could be more than two rates here in the future. The Standard Rate (15% at the time of writing) covers most consumer goods; and there is a Zero Rate which is applied to the 'necessities of life' such as food, fuel, children's clothes, books and newspapers, new houses and the post. It may seem a little pointless to charge a tax of 0%, but it is a reminder that many things are taxable if the Government of the day sees fit.

VAT is charged throughout the life of a product, for the theory is that each stage of its processing and handling *Adds Value* to it.

Thus:

Raw Materials	Cost £1 – VAT @ 15% Total Price £1.15
Manufactured Product	Cost £2 – VAT @ 15% Total Price £2.30
from the Wholesaler	Cost £3 + VAT @ 15% Total Price £3.45
at the Shop	Cost £5 + VAT @ 15% Total Price £5.75

Ultimately, it is only the end-user – the customer – who has to pay VAT. Everybody else along the line can usually claim back the VAT that they have paid; deducting it from the VAT that they have charged before handing the remainder on to the Customs & Excise.

The Materials Supplier		charges 15p	hands 15p to H.M.C.&E.
The Manufacturer	pays 15p	charges 30p	hands 15p to H.M.C.&E.
The Wholesaler	pays 30p	charges 45p	hands 15p to H.M.C.&E.
The Retailer	pays 45p	charges 75p	hands 30p to H.M.C.&E.
The Customer	pays 75p		

For any business involved in the VAT chain, two things are important. First, that the accounts relating to VATable transactions are kept with scrupulous accuracy, for H.M. Customs & Excise are very demanding in this respect; and secondly that the business claims back all the tax to which it is entitled. Fortunately there are no conflicts between these two goals.

Sundry Considerations

Businesses fall into four categories with respect to VAT.

Taxable firms charge VAT at Standard Rate on their goods or services. This Output Tax, less any Input Tax which they have paid, is sent to the tax authorities.

Zero Rated firms charge VAT at 0% on their products, but they are entitled to reclaim any VAT that they have paid. Publishers, builders and those in the food trades are in this happy position.

Partly Exempt firms supply goods or services at both Standard and Zero Rates. (They may also supply some which are tax exempt.) It is important for them to keep a clear distinction between the types.

Exempt firms do not charge VAT at all, and are not allowed to reclaim VAT. Insurance companies and banks are in this position, but so are the many small traders, craftsmen and professionals whose turnover is below the VAT threshold.

If an exempt business buys an item for £100 + VAT £15 (£115) and sells it for £145 with no VAT, its profit is only £30 for it cannot recover the £15 tax that it paid. The positive side to this is that the firm can keep its prices a little lower than if it was Taxable. Take that same £100 item and sell it through a Taxable firm and what happens? If there is to be a profit of £30, the sale price must be £130 to which VAT will add another £19.50 (£150 * 15%) – a total of £149.50.

Firms which are exempt because of their small turnover can normally opt for VAT registration if they wish.

The Treatment of VAT in the Accounts

There are certain conventions which are the same for both Sales and Purchases, and for allowable expenses.

Taxable Amount
The Nett Price is the final price after all discounts have been made. If the seller offers a discount for prompt payment – say 5% for settlement within fourteen days – then this must be deducted before VAT is calculated. Even if the buyer does not in the end qualify for the discount, the VAT will remain at the original (discounted) level. For example,

Sundry Considerations

```
                    Mercurian Pulp Products
                           Lennox House
                           Banister Park
                           Southampton
Sagesoft                                      Date 27/6/87
NEI House                                     Invoice No. 870231
Gosforth                                      Your Order No. 4529
Newcastle upon Tyne

                              INVOICE
                                                    £
        50 copies Easi-Calc system disks @ £15.00   750.00
       100 copies Taking Account manuals @ £12.50 1,250.00
                                                  ────────
                                                  2,000.00
                   Less Trade Discount 20%          400.00
                                                  ────────
                                                  1,600.00
       (1)         Add VAT @ 15%                    216.00
                                                  ────────
                                                  1,816.00
                                                  ════════
           Terms 10% discount 14 days settlement
```

1 If the bill is paid within fourteen days, the early settlement discount will reduce the pre-tax total to £1,440. VAT is calculated on this, *not* on the total shown (£1,440 * 15% = £216).

Nett prices are recorded in the Sales and Purchase accounts.
Gross prices are recorded in the suppliers' and customers' accounts.

The Tax Control Account
All VAT amounts – on both Inputs (Purchases) and Outputs (Sales) are recorded in a single Tax Control account. Its balance will be either a Current Asset or a Liability depending upon the levels of Input and Output Tax during the accounting period.

Credit Transactions
With credit transactions, VAT is normally due from the date of the sale or purchase, not from the date of payment. It can mean that where an invoice is raised in one quarter but not paid until the next, the seller will have to pay VAT to the Customs & Excise before it has been received. As the business is allowed a month after the end of a quarter before the VAT Return is due, this situation will only arise with very slow payers.

Sundry Considerations

With Purchases, the tax authorities have always allowed businesses to account for VAT at the date of payment rather than invoice. This may simplify the entries in a Cash Book accounting system, but it is poor practice from the point of view of the cash flow. There is no advantage in allowing a VAT claim to drift over into the following VAT period.

As from October 1987, the new *Cash Accounting Scheme* will enable smaller businesses to account for VAT on Sales (as well as Purchases) at the time of payments rather than invoices. This will be particularly advantageous to those firms that supply goods and services on extended credit. We will return to this scheme later.

Invoice Based VAT Accounting

When a *Sales Invoice* is raised, the Gross Price is entered as a Debit on the customer's account, while the Credit entries are split between Sales and Vat Control:

    Debit Customer Account   – Gross Price
    Credit Sales Account   – Nett Price
    Credit VAT Account   – VAT amount

A *Sales Credit Note* will need the opposite entries, except that the Nett Price will be a debit in Sales Returns, not Sales.

    Credit Customer Account   – Gross Price
    Debit Sales Returns   – Nett Price
    Debit VAT Account   – VAT amount

A *Sales Receipt* is recorded in exactly the same way as it is where there is no VAT. The tax has been taken care of at the Invoice stage.

    Credit Customer Account   – Gross Price
    Debit Cash/Bank Account   – Gross Price

In a *Cash Sale*, the Invoice and Receipt stages are telescoped into one.

    Credit Sales Account   – Nett Price
    Credit VAT Account   – VAT amount
    Debit Cash/ Bank Account   – Gross Price

Sundry Considerations

Credit and cash purchases are treated in corresponding ways. They can be summarised:

Purchase Invoice:

    Credit Supplier Account   – Gross Price
    Debit Purchases   – Nett Price
    Debit VAT Account   – VAT amount

Purchase Credit Note

    Debit Supplier Account   – Gross Price
    Credit Purchase Returns   – Nett Price
    Credit VAT Account   – VAT amount

Purchase Payment

    Debit Supplier Account   – Gross Price
    Credit Cash/ Bank Account   – Gross Price

Cash Purchase

    Debit Purchases   – Nett Price
    Debit VAT Account   – VAT amount
    Credit Cash/ Bank Account   – Gross Price

We can see this in practice if we take the following set of transactions and examine the relevant accounts at the end.

1. 5th April   Credit sale to Black & Smith (Ironmongers) £200 + VAT
2. 7th April   Credit purchase from Wheeler's Motors £100 + VAT
3. 10th April Cash sales of £50 + VAT
4. 12th April Returns, value £60 + VAT from Black & Smith
5. 14th April Cash purchase value £40 – VAT
6. 17th April Purchase returns value £20 + VAT to Wheeler's
7. 20th April Cheque from Black & Smith to settle bill
8. 21st April Cheque sent to Wheeler's to settle bill

Sundry Considerations

BLACK & SMITH

	£		£
5 April Sales	230.00	12 April Returns	69.00
		20 April Bank	161.00
	230.00		230.00

SALES ACCOUNT

	£		£
		5 April Black & Smith	200.00
		10 April Cash sales	50.00

SALES RETURNS ACCOUNT

	£		£
12 April Black & Smith	69.00		

WHEELER'S MOTORS

	£		£
17 April Purchase Returns	23.00	7 April Purchases	115.00
21 April Bank	92.00		
	115.00		115.00

PURCHASES ACCOUNT

	£		£
7 April Wheelers	100.00		
7 April Wheelers	100.00		
14 April Cash	40.00		

PURCHASE RETURNS ACCOUNT

	£		£
		17 April Wheelers	20.00

VAT CONTROL ACCOUNT

	£		£
7 April Wheelers	15.00	5 April Black & Smith	30.00
12 April Black & Smith	3.00	10 April Cash sales	7.50
Balance	20.50	14 April Wheelers	3.00
	40.50		40.50
		Balance	14.50

Sundry Considerations

The transfer to computer

The Sage accountancy packages designed for the PCW machine and those for PCs are identical in their structure and in the way that they handle VAT, but there are some minor differences of style – mainly in the use of the keyboard and in reference codes. The PC versions are used in this book, but the PCW equivalents will be readily found in the appropriate User Manuals.

All Sage accountancy packages are designed to cope with up to ten different rates of VAT. These are called up at need by using the codes T0 to T9. At the time of writing, the PC systems are being supplied to users with four 'active' codes, to suit the current VAT position. T0 is used for Zero Rated transactions, T1 for those at the Standard (15%) rate, T2 for exempt items and T9 for those transactions not subject to tax – such as the transfer of sums between accounts within the firm. The tax rates and the reference codes can be altered as needed, via the Tax Changes routine on the Utilities menu.

When Sales or Purchase Invoices are recorded, the system assumes that the value given as the Nett price is the pre-tax one. When you enter the tax code, the appropriate tax amount will be calculated on this basis. The VAT inclusive value will then be added to the Batch Total that is displayed at the top of the screen.

However, if the price you have is VAT-inclusive, there is no need for you to work out the nett price as Financial Controller can cope with this. Enter the gross price in the Nett column and then press [<]. The system will deduct the VAT for you. Thus, if you had received a Purchase Invoice for £230 (including VAT at 15%); enter £230 in the nett column, press [<] and the software will write £200 in the nett column and £30 under Tax. The Batch Total will still show £230.

If the VAT amount is different from that calculated by the system – an early settlement discount would reduce VAT – then the tax figure can be overwritten. An invoice which includes items at different tax rates should be split, if possible, into separate entries for each rate.

When the invoices are posted, the software will write up the accounts in much the same way as in a manual system. For example, when posting a Sales Invoice, the Invoice total is recorded in the Customer Account in the Sales Ledger, then in the Nominal Ledger:

Sundry Considerations

The Gross price is debited from the Debtors' Control Account
The Nett price is credited to the Sales Account
The VAT amount is credited to the Tax Control Account

When payment is received, the whole amount is marked off in the Customer Account, credited to Debtors' Control and debited from the Bank Account. There is no need for any special treatment of VAT at this stage, as it was fully recorded during Invoicing.

The treatment of non-credit sales and purchases is the same in Sage accounting as in a manual system. In both Cash and Bank Payments and Receipts, the software assumes — as it does for Invoices — that the Nett value is the pre-tax value. When the tax code is given, the appropriate VAT amount is calculated, written into the Tax column and added to the Batch Total. If the figure you have is for the VAT-inclusive value, then pressing [<] will deduct VAT from the amount given in the Nett column.

When a Cash Receipt is posted by the Sage package, it will make these entries to the accounts in the Nominal Ledger.

```
Credit Sales Account         – Nett Price
Credit Tax Control Account   – VAT amount
Debit Cash Account           – Gross Price
```

The Cash Accounting Scheme

As from Autumn 1987, all Sage accountancy packages will have the facilities to cope with this scheme, and upgrades will be offered to existing users if they wish to switch over to the new VAT system.

Under it, VAT will be charged on Sales Receipts and Purchase Payments, and not on Invoices. The effect on the accounts can be seen by following a credit sale through the system.

When the invoice is raised, the Nett amount and VAT will be recorded in the customer's account as normal. The software will then make the two entries:

```
Debit Debtors' Control    – Nett Price
Credit Sales              – Nett Price
```

Sundry Considerations

When a Sales Receipt is processed, the entries will be:

Debit Bank	– Gross Amount
Credit Debtors' Control	– Nett Amount
Credit Tax Control	– VAT amount

A cash sale would be recorded as under the existing system.

The VAT Return

The VAT Return routine in the Management Reports will give a tax analysis of all transactions in the Sales, Purchase and Nominal Ledgers. It also produces a summary showing the totals of the Inputs, Outputs and Tax under each code. The figures needed for the VAT Return can be extracted from these very readily, and the Tax Control account should show the balance due to or repayable by Customs & Excise.

The User Manual is very good in its treatment of the VAT routines, and should be consulted for detailed guidance.

Sundry Considerations

Depreciation

Here we are not concerned with how the depreciation of fixed assets should be handled in the accounts – that has already been covered earlier – but rather with the ways in which depreciation can be calculated.

Before any meaningful calculations can be made, three things must be known:

- The cost of the asset.

- The useful life of the asset. This will normally be expressed in terms of years though it may be more appropriate to measure it in terms of usage. The 'life-span' of a vehicle may be 200,000 miles, whether it takes two or ten years to reach that total. A machine may have a working life of 10,000 hours, but if it is only needed for certain tasks it may clock up 500 hours one year and 5,000 the next.

- The residual value at the end of its life. This will of necessity be an estimate, especially if the life-span is long and rates of inflation unpredictable. It is generally best to err on the side of caution, and use the lowest estimate. If that is all that the asset does realise when it is disposed of, then the cost will have been fully borne by depreciation over time. If it fetches more than was hoped, then this is a bonus to add to the year's profit.

There are two commonly used ways of calculating depreciation.

The Straight Line Method

In this method, the asset is depreciated by a fixed amount for each accounting period or unit of use. The amount is found by taking the loss on the item (Cost – Residual Value) and dividing it by the life.

For example, where the life is expressed in years:

Asset: Set of waiting room chairs
Cost: £1,000
Useful life: 4 years
Residual value: £200
Annual Depreciation: $\dfrac{£(1,000 - 200)}{4} = \dfrac{£800}{4} = £200$

Sundry Considerations

Where units of usage are used:

> Asset: Delivery lorry
> Cost: £10,000
> Useful life: 200,000 miles
> Residual Value: £2,000
> Depreciation per mile: $\dfrac{£(10,000 - 2,000)}{200,000} = \dfrac{£8,000}{200,000} = 4p$

In this case it would be better to express depreciation as £40 per 1,000 miles, so that the figures remain in round numbers. Useful life and Residual Value are both estimates, so the calculation cannot possibly be accurate. Mileage should also be rounded to the nearest 1,000 when working out the sum.

If the lorry had covered 25,273 miles during the year, this would be taken as 25,000 miles, giving a depreciation for the year of:

> 25 * £40 = £1,000

Compare this with the one obtained by 'accurate' calculation:

> 25,273 * 4p = 101,092p = £1010.92

Which is more meaningful?

The Reducing Balance Method

This method works by reducing the asset value by a fixed percentage, and not a fixed sum of money, each year. So, if a computer was purchased for £4,000 and depreciated at a rate of 50% p.a., this pattern would emerge:

Sundry Considerations

	Cost new	£4,000
Year 1	Depreciation 50% * £4,000	£2,000
	End of year value	£2,000
Year 2	Depreciation 50% * £2,000	£1,000
	End of year value	£1,000
Year 3	Depreciation 50% * £1,000	£500
	End of year value	£500
Year 4	Depreciation 50% * £500	£250
	End of year value	£250

If the computer did have a useful life of four years and a residual value of £250, then the Straight Line method would have given an annual depreciation of approximately £950. This would put its value at the end of Year 1 at over £3,000, which could well prove to be far more than anyone would be willing to pay for a second-hand computer.

The percentage to use for the depreciation can be found by the formula:

$$\frac{P}{100} = 1 - \sqrt[N]{\frac{\text{Residual Value}}{\text{Cost}}}$$

'P' is the percentage and 'N' the number of years of useful life. Finding the Nth root of a fraction is near-enough impossible by hand, but easily accomplished with a spreadsheet or a pocket calculator.

For example, the asset costs £1,000, has a useful life of four years and a residual value of £200. The formula gives us:

$$\frac{P}{100} = 1 - \sqrt[4]{\frac{200}{1000}} = 33\% \text{ (approx.)}$$

(The fourth root of 0.2 is fractionally lower than 0.67, but the figures have been rounded here and in the following example so that the pattern is more visible.)

Sundry Considerations

The depreciation costs over the life would work out as shown here.

	Cost new	£1,000
Year 1	Depreciation 33% * £1,000	£330
	End of year value	£670
Year 2	Depreciation 33% * £670	£221
	End of year value	£449
Year 3	Depreciation 33% * £449	£149
	End of year value	£300
Year 4	Depreciation 33% * £300	£100
	End of year value	£200

The Straight Line method has the advantage of being easy to implement, and works very well if the asset concerned is retained for the full term of its estimated life. The disadvantage is that it is not very realistic. An asset will normally lose value faster during the first few years. We only have to walk around a second-hand car showroom to become aware of this. A new car may drop in value by £3,000 in its first year, but there will be a negligible difference in price between a seven-year old and an eight-year old car.

If it is possible that the asset will be disposed of before the end of its useful life, then the Reducing Balance method should be used. That way the disposal value is less likely to be significantly different from the depreciated value.

Sundry Considerations

The Treatment of Hire Purchase

Whether a business is selling goods or buying items – normally fixed assets – on hire purchase, the accounting treatment remains much the same in a number of ways.

In legal terms the ownership of an article does not pass to the buyer until all of the instalments have been paid, but in accountancy terms it is the substance, not the form, that matters. The article is treated as if it had become the property of the buyer from the start of the agreement. The seller will record a sale, and the buyer will open accounts for the asset and its depreciation. Both will use the cash price of the item and ignore the interest in these accounts.

The financing of the sale or purchase is handled through a hire purchase account. The original cost, the interest charge and the payments will be recorded here.

We will take the purchase of an industrial cooker and look at the accounts from both sides. It is priced at £1,000 cash, or £280 deposit and 24 monthly payments of £40 – a total hire-purchase price of £1,240.

The Buyer

Heather bought the new cooker as part of her expansion programme, from Clements Catering Supplies. As it happens, the purchase took place at the start of her financial year – which will make the calculations simpler. She opened two new accounts – one marked 'Cooker' and one marked 'Hire Purchase'. A third account for depreciation would also be need to be opened at some point during the year.

The acquisition was recorded by a Credit entry in Hire Purchase and a Debit in the Cooker account. No further entries are needed in that latter account. The deposit and the monthly instalment payments were recorded as Debits in the Hire Purchase account; and at the end of the year the interest charge – for that year only – was recorded as a Credit there. It is important to note that the interest charge is spread evenly over the period of the agreement and credited year by year. In this case, the total interest is £240, or £120 p.a.

The relevant accounts at the end of the first year are shown here.

Sundry Considerations

COOKER ACCOUNT

	£			£
1 Jan Hire Purchase	1,000.00	31 Dec	Balance	1,000.00
	1,000.00			1,000.00
Balance b/f	1,000.00			

HIRE PURCHASE ACCOUNT

	£			£
1 Jan Deposit	280.00	1 Jan	Cooker	1,000.00
31 Dec Bank a/c		31 Dec	Profit & Loss a/c	
12 * £40 payments	480.00		Interest	120.00
Balance	360.00			
	1120.00			1,120.00
			Balance b/f	360.00

During the following year, another £120 interest will be charged to the hire purchase account, bringing its Credit total to £480. This will be balanced by the £480 from the last twelve instalments.

Year 2   HIRE PURCHASE ACCOUNT

	£			£
		1 Jan	Cooker Balance	360.00
31 Dec Bank a/c		31 Dec	Profit & Loss a/c	
12 * £40 payments	480.00		Interest	120.00
	480.00			480.00

Notice that in the Hire Purchase account, the interest is labelled 'Profit & Loss a/c'. In a manual system it is perfectly feasible to make debit or credit entries directly into the Profit and Loss account. It exists on the ledger pages, just as the other accounts do. You cannot make this kind of direct entry in a computerised system, for the Profit and Loss Account does not exist as a separate entity. It is a collection of other accounts, and only appears as a whole when printed out on paper. It will therefore be necessary to set up an Interest account, within the Expenses area, to record the debit entry. While all payments can be made through the Bank Payments routine, the other transactions will have to be handled via Journal Entries.

Sundry Considerations

Summary For A Computerised System

At the start of the hire purchase term:

> OPEN Accounts in the Nominal Ledger for the Asset, Hire Purchase and Interest.
>
> Use Journal Entries to Debit Asset and Credit Hire Purchase with the Cash Price.
>
> Use Bank Payments to Credit Bank and Debit Hire Purchase with the Deposit.

At the end of each instalment period (normally monthly):

> Use Bank Payments to Credit Bank and Debit Hire Purchase with the Instalment.

At the end of the financial year:

> Use Journal Entries to Debit Interest and Credit Hire Purchase with the Year's interest.

The Vendor

Clements Catering Supplies sell goods for cash and on hire purchase. This is financed from within the firm, rather than through a Finance Company, as it has the resources to extend credit to its customers and as the interest charges are an additional source of profit.

It buys in industrial cookers for £800 each, and thus earns a Gross profit of £200 on a simple cash sale. Where the sale is on hire purchase, the profit is worked out as follows:

	£
Deposit	280
Instalments (24 * £40)	960
Total price	1,240
Cost	800
Profit	440

173

Sundry Considerations

This profit has two distinct components:

	£
Gross trading profit	200
Hire purchase interest	240
Total Profit	440

This split is reflected in the way that the transaction is handled in the vendor's accounts. Three accounts are used – the normal Sales account; and two new ones marked 'H.P. Interest' (or similar) and 'Hire Purchase Debtors'.

Cash Price	Credit Sales	Debit H.P. Debtors'
Interest	Credit H.P. Interest	Debit H.P. Debtors'

The deposit and the subsequent instalments are all entered as Credits in the hire purchase Debtors' account, balanced by Debits in Bank or Cash. We can follow this over the period of the loan. The situation is made a little more complicated by the fact that Clements Catering's accounting year starts in May.

HIRE PURCHASE DEBTORS' ACCOUNT

			£				£
1 Jan	Sales		1,000.00	1 Jan	Bank a/c Deposit		280.00
1 Jan	H.P. Interest		240.00	30 Apr	Bank a/c 4 * £40		160.00
					Balance c/f		800.00
			1,240.00				1,240.00
Year 2							
	Balance b/f		800.00	30 Apr	Bank a/c 12 * £40		480.00
					Balance c/f		320.00
			800.00				800.00
Year 3							
	Balance b/f		320.00	30 Apr	Bank a/c 8 * £40		320.00

(For convenience, we have shown each year's payments as a single sum. In practice they would have been entered monthly.)

The sum that has been credited to the Hire Purchase Interest account is

Sundry Considerations

profit *but* it is a profit that must be spread over the term of the payments. Only the portion that has been 'earned' in an accounting year can be included in the Profit and Loss Account. The remainder will appear in the Balance Sheet as a Current Asset, as it will become profit in the future.

The simplest method of spreading the interest is to find what fraction of the instalments were received during that year and multiply this by the total interest. In this example, there would have been four payments by the end of Clements' accounting year, so the finance profit would have been 4 / 24 * £240 = £40. The balance of £200 is carried forward into the next year.

H.P. INTEREST ACCOUNT

```
                                    £                                    £
                                         1 Jan H.P.Debtors           240.00
30 Apr Profit & Loss a/c
       4 / 24 * 240            40.00
       Balance c/f            200.00
                              ──────                                 ──────
                              240.00                                 240.00
                              ══════                                 ══════
Year 2
                                         Balance b/f                 200.00
30 Apr Profit & Loss a/c
       12 / 24 * 240          120.00
       Balance c/f             80.00
                              ──────                                 ──────
                              200.00                                 200.00
                              ══════                                 ══════
Year 3
                                         Balance b/f                  80.00
30 Apr Profit & Loss a/c
       8 / 24 * 240            80.00
                              ══════                                 ══════
```

As we noted earlier in this section, it is not possible to write entries directly into the Profit and Loss Account of Financial Controller. When transferring to that system, therefore, a new account will be needed within the Profit and Loss area. It could be labelled 'Finance Profit'.

At the end of the accounting period the earned portion will be debited from Hire Purchase Interest and credited to this account. Finance Profit would then be included in an 'Overhead' category in the Profit and Loss account – as it is a credit balance it will contribute to the Nett Profit; and Hire Purchase Interest will be written into the Current Assets on the Balance Sheet.

Sundry Considerations

Summary For A Computerised System

At the start of hire purchase term:

> OPEN Accounts in the Nominal Ledger for Hire Purchase Debtors, Interest and Finance Profits.
>
> Use the normal Invoice routines to Credit Sales and Debit H.P. Debtors with the Cash Price.
>
> Use Journal Entries to Credit Interest and Debit Hire Purchase Debtors with all the Interest.
>
> Use Bank Receipts to Debit Bank and Credit Hire Purchase Debtors with the Deposit.

At the end of each instalment period (normally monthly):

> Use Bank Receipts to Debit Bank and Credit Hire Purchase Debtors with the Instalment.

At the end of the financial year:

> Use Journal Entries to Debit Interest and Credit Finance Profit with the Year's interest.

7

Accountancy Software and your accounts

Anyone who runs a business knows that the integrity of the accounts is of vital importance. Errors and omissions create extra work – and it can take countless hours to track down even one mistake when you are trying to balance the books at the end of the year. Lost or damaged accounts are almost irreplaceable – they will cause problems with the tax and VAT authorities and could cost money in unclaimed debts and unrecorded expenses. And as we have seen, the accounts can be used to paint a picture of the profitability and progress of the business. Incomplete accounts will leave blank areas in that picture.

Any major changes in an existing accounting system – and computerisation is a major change – should therefore be approached thoughtfully and cautiously, testing each stage before moving on to a deeper commitment and ensuring that each concept and operation is fully understood before it is actually put into practice.

Accountancy Software and your Accounts

Organising your Accounts

Where the accounts are handled solely through a two-column cash book, or one of the proprietory single-entry accounts books, the first stage is to think in terms of double entries and of separate accounts for each type of transaction.

You may at present be noting the date and value of transactions in the Cash book, with descriptions such as 'Cash Sales', 'Cheque from B.Wilmot – on the *in* side – and 'Petrol', 'Typewriter Ribbons', 'Stamps', 'Cleaning Materials', '500 Widgets from M.P.P.(paid)' – on the *out*. It is an adequate system for a small firm, and takes very little time to maintain on a day to day basis. However, at the end of the year you would need to spend time working through the book, collecting all the ins and outs into convenient categories for the final accounts – or more likely, you would leave an accountant to do that job.

If you are already using double-entry book-keeping, then a system of accounts will already exist; but the time of transfer to computer is a good time for taking stock of the way you handle your accounts. Is there room for improvement in your system? Does it give you all the information you need for effective management – and remember that you can store more information and handle it more easily on a computer. (Remember also that it is just as easy to store irrelevant information which will confuse rather than enlighten.)

The basic accounting structure should, therefore, be comprehensive, but no more detailed than necessary. One Sales and one Purchases account will be enough where all goods are of a similar type, but where there are distinctly different types and it is useful to keep track of the volume and profitability of each, then separate accounts should be used.

Similarly, expenses should be grouped sensibly, avoiding a multiplicity of accounts, each recording very small sums. There is normally little point in recording separately those sums spent on pens, paper, envelopes, and typewriter (or printer) ribbons – 'Stationery' should cover them all. And if very little is spent on stationery, then the costs could be included in a wider category of Office Expenses, or of General Expenses.

The key consideration here is to strike a balance between convenience and cost control. The more (smaller) accounts you have, the more cluttered the ledgers will be and the more time it will take to maintain and analyse the data; but it will be easier to see how money is being spent

Accountancy Software and your Accounts

– and therefore where it may be possible to make economies. For instance, if the Telephone bills are included in the Office Expenses account, they are not as 'visible' as they are in a separate account. They won't appear in the Trial Balance or any of the end of period reports. Escalating bills – which should be investigated immediately – may not therefore be noticed until they have run on for some time.

All of the accounts discussed so far will fall within the Nominal Ledger of either a manual or a computerised system. If there are regular customers and suppliers with whom the business trades on credit, then there should be accounts for these – but within the Sales and Purchases Ledgers. They do not all need to be set up at once. New accounts can be opened at any time.

Where credit transactions are few or insignificant in value, then it is possible to bypass these ledgers – perhaps bringing them in at a later date. As long as you are not VAT-registered, there is nothing to stop you keeping sales and purchase invoices to one side and only entering the transactions into the accounts when the bills are paid. VAT-registered traders could also do this, but they would have to make sure that for VAT purposes the invoices were included in the period in which they were issued, and not in which they were paid.

The Transfer to the Computer

Switching the accounts from a manual system to a computerised one will inevitably cause some upheaval, and it will always involve some extra work – if only in installing the software for the business and typing in the account details. With careful planning the upheaval and extra work can be kept to a minimum.

Get to know the software before you start to do anything serious with it. But before you do anything at all, take three full copies of the master disks. You will need one set for experimentation, one for actual use in the business and one in case the first attempts at installation go wrong, or the disks are damaged in some way. Put the master disks, the working copy and the back-up copy safely to one side for the time being while you 'play' with the experimentation set.

Set up a dummy business and work through a representative sequence of transactions – a month's trading from one of our sample businesses should serve as a basis for this. This will give you a chance to get the feel of what is happening, spot the mistakes that are likely to occur and learn how to correct them. Keep experimenting until you are sure that you can handle all the types of transactions that will occur in your business. Bring in those memebers of staff who will be operating the new system and show them how it works. Let them use the dummy accounts to practise their new roles. Only when you, and they, are confident about the use of the software should you start the process of transferring the real accounts to the computer.

You will need to make some changes to the office to accommodate the computer. The physical rearrangements may have already been done, but will be the least troublesome part of this anyway. What will need more thought are the changes that must be made to office practices – the methods of data collection and entry and the end of day routines when the system is closed down and back-up copies are made of the data disks. Even with a hard disk system, you should take regular back-up copies of the data files on floppies as the hard disk could be corrupted by a power failure.

It must be stressed that the transfer should not be a sudden switch from manual to computer. The existing manual system must be run alongside the computer one until you are sure that the new system is being used properly. It may well mean that doing the accounts takes almost twice as long for a month or more, but the alternative is far worse. How much work will it take to sort out the mess if things go wrong? With Sage accounts packages, the software itself is reliable, and the Amstrad PCs and PCWs are unlikely to break down, but disk damage is always a possibility and human errors are all too common in any new system.

A full month is an absolute minimum for this phase-in time. You must reach the point of producing end-of-period reports, so that the outputs from the two systems can be compared. Ideally you would run the twin systems for the last few months of the financial year. This would give you time to sort out any problems and allow you to start the new year fully computerised and fully confident.

It makes a great deal of sense to take a piecemeal approach – though keeping the final goal in mind. Start with that aspect of the accounts which can be transferred most easily and which is least likely to cause problems if there are hitches in the computer system.

There are two alternative ways of making a stage by stage transfer.

Accountancy Software and your Accounts

Where the business is organised into several departments, or where there are distinct areas of operation, one department or area could be computerised while the rest continue to run a manual-only system. This would give staff a chance to familiarise themselves with the use of the computer and the software, and management the opportunity to study the effectiveness of the system.

The other approach — and the one that is probably most suitable for smaller businesses — is to use only part of the accountancy package in the beginning. The Nominal Ledger can be used by itself, as can the Stock Control module — and here you could start with only part of the inventory on the computer. It would be possible to start by focusing on either the Sales or Purchases Ledger, though key Nominal accounts — Creditors' and Debtors' Control, Bank, Discount and VAT — would also be needed for this.

SUMMARY

- Take three full copies of the Sage disks.

- Get to know the software.

- Develop the accounting structure.

- Arrange the office and plan working habits.

- Make sure that everyone understands their new roles.

- Phase in the software, alongside the existing system.

- Keep part, or all, of the manual system in operation until you are confident that its computer equivalent is running smoothly.

- Reap the benefits of reduced clerical time, more efficient operations and better management information.

Glossary

Accrual An amount of money owing for a specific expense at the end of an accounting period. e.g. Electricity – Paid £400, Accrued £100 gives a total cost of £500 for the period.

Amortisation Spreading the cost of an intangible asset, such as a lease, over the years in which it is enjoyed. Depreciation serves the same cost-spreading function for tangible assets like machines and vehicles.

Appropriation Accounts Show the way that the nett profit is distributed between partners, or between shareholders and reserve funds in a company.

Asset Something owned by the business. Fixed Assets will normally be retained for at least a year; Current Assets will be realised in the shorter term.

Audit Trail The way in which auditors follow logically through the course of events as recorded in the accounts. In Sage accountancy packages, the Audit Trail gives print-outs of transactions in date order.

Authorised Share Capital The total value of shares that the company could issue, as distinct from the Called-up and Paid-up Share Capital.

Glossary

Bad Debt An outstanding debt which the business believes will never be paid.

Balance Sheet Shows the total Assets and Liabilities of the business and explains the way in which the activities have been financed.

Book Value The value at which an asset is recorded in the books of account. It may be the Historic Cost, the Net Realisable Value or the depreciated value.

Call When shares are issued, only part of their cost is usually paid at the time of application and allotment. A Call is a demand by the company for part or all of the outstanding sums to be paid.

Called-up Share Capital The face value of shares for which payment has been called, though not necessarily made.

Capital Employed In general, the money invested in the business. Shareholders' capital employed refers to share capital and reserves only; total capital employed includes long-term loans.

Capital Expenditure Money spent on the acquisition of an asset, such as premises, plant or machinery, that will be used within the business over a period of years.

Contra An exchange from one account to another. Most commonly used in a manual cash-book when money is transferred between Cash and Bank. The only reference given would be a 'C' in the Folio column.

Control Accounts A system of grouping similar account together so that errors can be localised. In Sage packages, there are control accounts for creditors, debtors, cash, bank, tax and discount.

Cost of Goods Sold Means precisely what it says. It refers only to goods which have actually been sold, and the cost includes purchase price and an appropriate share of overheads – or raw materials, direct and indirect expenses for a manufacturing firm.

Credit A right-hand entry in the double-entry system. Think of it as something going out of an account. Profit shows up as a credit, because this is going out of the year's accounts – into the owners' pockets!

Creditor A person or company to whom the business owes money.

Glossary

Current Asset E.g. Stock, debtors, prepayments, money in the bank or in cash. (*See Asset.*)

Current Liability e.g. creditor, accrual, overdraft. (*See Liability.*)

Day Books Daily record of transactions, e.g. Sales and Purchases. In the Sage systems, the Day Book routines give print-outs of transactions over a given period of time.

Debit A left-hand entry in the double-entry system. It records a gain made by an account.

Debtor A person or business who owes money to the business.

Depreciation An amount which is deducted from the value of an asset to spread its cost over its useful life-span.

Discount An amount by which a bill is reduced. Can be divided into Discount Allowed – given by the business, and Discount Received – given to the business. Both can be handled by a single account. In Sage Stock Control Modules, the discounts allowed on items are written into the Stock Control details. Up to three alternative discounts can be linked to each stock line.

Distributable Profits In company accounts these are the sums that are available for dividends to shareholders. While based on the Nett Profit, they may be increased by undistributed profits from the previous year, or reduced by the need to retain some for reserves.

Dividend The amount paid out per share. Usually described as a percentage of the face value (the original price) of one share. So, a 10% dividend on £1 share would be 10p.

Double-Entry Book-keeping A system of keeping accounts where each transaction is recorded as a debit entry in one account and a corresponding credit entry in a second.

Doubtful Debt or Provision for Bad Debt An amount put by for those debts which may not be paid. It appears as an expense in the Profit and Loss Account, and is deducted from the Debtors' Control.

Drawings Cash or goods taken from the business for the owner's personal use. Drawings do not count as an expense in the Profit and Loss

Glossary

Account, and must be included in the 'Financed by' section of the Balance Sheet.

Equity Capital   The money invested in a business by its owners.

Finance Profit   Profit on the interest charges of a hire purchase sale. Should be kept distinct from the Gross Profit.

Fixed Asset   E.g. buildings, plant and machinery, vehicles. (*See Asset.*)

Folio   In a manual system, the number which identifies a transaction. In the Sage accountancy systems, the Transaction Number serves the same purpose.

Fungible   Describes goods of the same type but different prices — presumably from different deliveries.

Gross Profit (Trading Profit)   Sales less Purchases less Direct Expenses. (*See Nett Profit.*)

Historic Cost   Original cost of an asset.

Intangible Asset   One which has no physical existence, e.g. goodwill, or the rights to royalty payments.

Inventory   Stock and Work in Progress.

Journal Entries   In the Sage systems, this refers to the recording of transactions by making both the debit and credit entries into the relevant (Nominal) accounts. This differs from Bank and Cash payments and receipts which require only a single entry by the user, with the balancing entry made by the system.

Liability   Something owed by the business. May be divided into Current Liabilites — those which must be paid within a year; and Long-term Liabilites such as bank loans.

Monetary Asset/Liability   Cash, Bank holdings or bank overdraft.

Nett Profit   Gross Profit less Expenses.

Nominal Ledger (General/Impersonal Ledger)   In a manual system, the book in which all accounts except Sales, Purchases and the Cash Book are kept. In the Sage systems, the Cash and Bank accounts are also in this ledger.

Opening Balance The amount written into an account at the start of an accounting period.

Operating Assets A concept mainly used in ratio analysis. The description is applied to those assets which are employed in generating profit through trading. This includes the business's premises, equipment, stock and debtors. Investments and cash are excluded.

Operating Profit Gross Profit less the expenses incurred in trade. It will be the same as the Nett Profit, unless the business has other income from investments, or expenditure on loan interest. These items are not considered in calculating the Operating Profit.

Overtrading Engaging in more activities than can be properly financed by the business.

Paid-up Share Capital That share capital for which all payments have been called up and made.

Prepayments A payment made in one accounting period for an expense that will be incurred in the next; e.g. where rent is paid quarterly in advance and there is still a month left at the end of the business's financial year. The prepayment is deducted from the expense in the Profit and Loss Account, and appears among the Current Assets in the Balance Sheet.

Profit and Loss Account Shows the expenses that are deducted from the Gross Profit to produce the Nett Profit.

Provision (for depreciation/bad debt) An estimated value written into the expenses. When an asset is finally disposed of, its actual cost over time can be compared with the provision made for its depreciation, and a correcting entry made. The 'final' cost of bad debts will not be known until the business ceases to trade, but experience will indicate the level that is needed.

Purchase Ledger A list of credit purchases over time, organised into accounts for each supplier.

Quick (Assets) Ratio Shows the liquidity of the business by comparing

Glossary

realisable current assets (cash, debtors and short-term investments) and liabilities (creditors, tax and short-term loans). Ideally the ratio should be at least 1:1, unless there are overdraft facilities. The limitation of the Sage system's Quick Ratio Report (in the Nominal Ledger section), is that is does not indicate the speed with which debtors will pay.

Ratio Analysis   Technique for examining the profitability and progress of a business by comparing selected figures from the accounts.

Reserve   A sum of money set aside for a future cost, such as the replacement of fixed assets.

Returns   Goods returned to the business, or by the business to the supplier. Recorded in Sage accounts packages via the Credit Note routines.

Revenue Expenditure   Money spent on things for use within the current accounting period.

Sale or Return   Goods supplied on the understanding that if not sold on (by the retailer) they may be returned without charge. Such transactions are best not recorded in the accounts until the actual sales figures are known.

Sales Ledger   A list of credit sales over a period of time, organised into customer accounts.

Stock Explosion   Not a sudden, enormous increase in the stocks held, but a breakdown of stock items into component parts. E.g. in a HiFi store, this would show turntables, amplifiers, loudspeakers, etc., as separate items rather than as the systems into which they are normally organised.

Suspense Account   When a Trial Balance fails to balance, the difference may be written into a temporary Suspense Account. The individual accounts are then checked for errors. When one is found, a correcting entry is made in the account, and a balancing one in the Suspense Account. Ultimately the balance in this should be reduced to zero.

Tangible Asset   A physical one, as opposed to an Intangible Asset.

Trading Account   Compares Sales, Stock used and Direct Expenses to find the profit or loss made by simply buying and selling.

Working Capital   Current assets minus current liabilities.

Index

Acid Test Ratio, 144
Account History, 43
Account Names, 41
Accounting Year, 45
Accruals, 111
 – in Sage systems, 115
Appropriation Accounts,
Partnership, 116
 – Limited Company, 123
 – in Sage systems, 121
Assets, 17
Authorised Share Capital, 133
AVCO, Stock Valuation, 136
Balance Sheet, 126
 – in Sage systems, 130
Balancing at end of month, 40
Bank Account, 21
Bank Payments, 43
Books of Account, 29
Capital, 19
Capital Account, 20
 – in Partnership, 55
 – in Limited Company, 67
Carriage Inwards, 57
Carriage Outwards, 59
Cash Account, 26
Cash Accounting Scheme for VAT, 165
Cash Book, 32
Cash Retailer, 11
Commissions, 69
Computerisation – at Start of Year, 41
 – Mid-Year Start, 62
Control Accounts, 42
Credit, 16
Credit Notes, 53
Creditors, 29
Current Asset, 17
 – in Balance Sheet, 127

Current Liabilities, 18
Current Ratio, 144
Day Books, 30
Debentures, 130
Debit, 16
Debtors, 30
Debtors' Control Account, 42
Depreciation Accounts, 74
 – Calculations, 167
 – in Balance Sheet, 127
Direct Costs of Production, 93
Directors' Fees, 70
Discount – Received, 74
 – Allowed, 76
 – Accounts in Sage systems, 79
Distributor, 11
Dividends, 123
Double-Entry Book-keeping, 15
Drawings – Sole trader, 39
 – Partnership, 60
 – Intereston, 117
Economic Order Quantity, 138
End of Period Adjustments, 110
 – in Sage systems, 115
Errors – minimising, 82
Expenses – Business & Private, 51
Factory Cost, 89
 – Overheads, 89
FIFO, Stock Valuation, 136
Financial Controller, 10
Financed By, Balance Sheet heading, 129
Fixed Asset, 17
General Ledger, 32
Gross Profit or Loss, 98
Grunks Ltd – First Month, 65
 – Trial Balance, 85
 – Manufacturing Account, 93

Index

- Trading Accounts, 102
Heather's Cafe – First Month, 34
 - Trial Balance, 83
 - Trading Account, 99
 - Profit & Loss Account, 106
Hire Purchase, 171
 - in Sage systems, 173
Impersonal Ledger, 32
Indirect Costs of Production, 93
Initialisation routine, 41
Journal Entries, 44
Ledger System, 29
Ledger Page, Left-Right Split, 16
Liabilities, 18
LIFO, Stock Valuation, 136
Limited Company, 64
Liquidity Ratios, 143
Manufacturer, 12
Manufacturing Account, 88
 - in Sage systems, 94
Mortgage Repayments, 56
Motor Vehicle Accounts, 68
Nett Profit or Loss, 104
Nominal Ledger, 32
Notes on the Accounts, 112
Opening Balances, 62
Ordinary Shares, 64
Over-depreciation, 114
Overheads, 89
Palfreman Motor Spares – First Month, 44
 - Trial Balance, 84
 - Trading Account, 100
 - Profit & Loss Account, 108
 - Ratio Analysis, 148
Partnerships, 54
 - Appropriation Account, 116
 - Capital, 55
 - Capital & Current Accounts, 119
 - Drawings, 60
 - Interest on Drawings, 117
 - Salaries, 118
Posting Transactions, 43

Preference Shares, 64
Prepayments, 112
 - in Sage systems, 115
Prime Cost of Production, 88
Production Cost of Goods, 89
Profit, Gross, 98
 - Nett, 104
 - Unappropriated, 123
 - Volume Ratio, 145
Profit & Loss Account, 104
 - in Sage systems, 109
Profitability Ratios, 144
Purchase Accounts, 29
 - Day Book, 30
 - Ledger, 29
 - Returns, 52
Quick Ratio, 144
Ratio Analysis, 143
Raw Materials, treated as Purchases, 68
 - Cost of, 90
Records of Account, 16
Reorder Level, 140
Returns – Inwards, 49
 - Outwards, 48
Reserves, 124
Safety Stock Level, 140
Sales Account, 26
 - Day Book, 30
 - Ledger, 30
 - Margin Ratio, 145
 - Returns, 52
Service Industries, 12
Share Capital, 64
 - Authorised, 133
Sole Trader, Balance Sheet, 129
Stock Control, 135
 - Closing, 90
 - Opening, 90
 - Valuation, 136
 - Explosion Report, 142
Sue's Salon – First Month, 73
 - Trial Balance, 86
 - Trading Account, 103

190

– Profit & Loss Account, 107
Sundry Creditors, 42
 – Debtors, 83
Suppliers' Accounts, 29
Tax Control Account, 42
Trading Account, 96
 – in Sage systems, 109
Trial Balance, 81
Two-Tone Cash & Carry – First Month, 54
 – Trial Balance, 84
 – Trading Account, 100
 – Profit & Loss Account, 106
 – Ratio Analysis, 152

Unappropriated Profit, 123
VAT, 157
 – Cash Accounting Scheme, 165
 – categories of business, 159
 – in Sage accountancy systems, 164
 – Return, 166
 – treatment in accounts, 159
 – where recorded, 42
Wholesaler, 12
Work in Progress, 89
Working Capital, 19